"One of the top plays of the year . . . Brechtian allegory and Homeric epic in an essential American tragedy."

D0373345

"By turns philosophical and playful, lyrical and earthy, *Father Comes Home from the Wars (Parts 1, 2 & 3)* swoops, leaps, dives and soars, reimagining a turbulent turning point in American history through a cockeyed contemporary lens . . . The wonder of Ms. Parks's achievement is how smoothly she blends the high and the low, the serious and the humorous, the melodramatic and the grittily realistic."

—Charles Isherwood, *New York Times*

"Suzan-Lori Parks's stunning new drama is that rare work of art: one that bears the heavy burden of its subject matter—the peculiar institution of American slavery—but that carries it lightly . . . Parks brings the full force of her dramatic power. She both elevates her themes with echoes of classic literature, while at the same time doubling down on comedy . . . This is serious work that is seriously entertaining."

—Thom Geier, *Entertainment Weekly*

"The best new play of the year . . . It is bold, hugely entertaining, moving and thrillingly ambitious. Suzan-Lori Parks bids fair to create a sprawling multi-part epic to plant alongside August Wilson's monumental Century Cycle, one of the great achievements in theater history. Parts 4 through 9 (or more?) can't come fast enough."

—Michael Giltz, *Huffington Post*

"Suzan-Lori Parks may reach back to the ancient Greeks for references and structure, but her play delivers an in-the-moment gut punch. *Father Comes Home from the Wars* is an insightful, poetic, often heartbreaking look at the devastations of war and slavery and the complications of freedom."

—Robert Feldberg, *Bergen Record*

FATHER COMES HOME FROM THE WARS

PARTS 1, 2 & 3

**Other Books by Suzan-Lori Parks
Published by TCG**

The America Play and Other Works
   Also Includes:
   Essays
   Imperceptible Mutabilities in the Third Kingdom
   Betting on the Dust Commander
   Pickling
   The Death of the Last Black Man in the Whole Entire World
   Devotees in the Garden of Love

The Book of Grace

The Red Letter Plays
   Includes:
   Fucking A
   In the Blood

365 Days/365 Plays

Topdog/Underdog

Venus

FATHER COMES HOME FROM THE WARS

PARTS 1, 2 & 3

Suzan-Lori Parks

Theatre Communications Group
New York
2015

Father Comes Home from the Wars (Parts 1, 2 & 3) is published by Theatre Communications Group, Inc., 520 Eighth Avenue, 24th Floor, New York, NY 10018-4156

The publication of *Father Comes Home from the Wars (Parts 1, 2 & 3)*, by Suzan-Lori Parks, through TCG's Book Program, is made possible in part by the New York State Council on the Arts with the support of Governor Andrew Cuomo and the New York State Legislature.

TCG books are exclusively distributed to the book trade by Consortium Book Sales and Distribution.

Library of Congress Cataloging-in-Publication Data
Parks, Suzan-Lori.
Father comes home from the wars (parts 1, 2 & 3) / Suzan-Lori Parks.
pages ; cm
ISBN 978-1-55936-500-0 (softcover)
ISBN 978-1-55936-817-9 (ebook)
1. Slaves—United States—Drama. 2. United States—History—Civil War, 1861–1865—Drama. I. Title.
PS3566.A736F38   2015
812'.54—dc23   2015001459

Book design and composition by Lisa Govan
Cover design by JB and Kitty Suen
Front cover: Sterling K. Brown as Hero; back cover: Louis Cancelmi as Smith (The Public Theater production). Photos by Tammy Shell

First Edition, May 2015
Fourth Printing, September 2020

Returning is the Way of the Tao.

—Tao Te Ching, Verse XL

Contents

Production History

Father Comes Home from the Wars (Parts 1, 2 & 3) was first produced at The Public Theater (Oskar Eustis, Artistic Director; Patrick Willingham, Executive Director) in New York City on October 28, 2014. The director was Jo Bonney; the set design was by Neil Patel, the costume design was by ESosa, the lighting design was by Lap Chi Chu, the sound design was by Dan Moses Schreier, the songs and additional music were by Suzan-Lori Parks, the music was arranged and performed by Steven Bargonetti; the production stage manager was Evangeline Rose Whitlock. The cast was:

The Musician	Steven Bargonetti

Part 1: A Measure of a Man
The Chorus of Less Than Desirable Slaves:

Leader	Russell G. Jones
Second	Julian Rozzell Jr.
Third	Tonye Patano
Fourth	Jacob Ming-Trent
The Oldest Old Man	Peter Jay Fernandez
Hero	Sterling K. Brown
Penny	Jenny Jules
Homer	Jeremie Harris

Part 2: A Battle in the Wilderness

A Colonel, In the Rebel Army	Ken Marks
Smith, A captive Union soldier	Louis Cancelmi
Hero, The Colonel's slave	Sterling K. Brown

Part 3: The Union of My Confederate Parts

The Runaway Slaves	Russell G. Jones, Tonye Patano and Julian Rozzell Jr.
Homer	Jeremie Harris
Penny	Jenny Jules
Odyssey Dog	Jacob Ming-Trent
Ulysses	Sterling K. Brown

This production of *Father Comes Home from the Wars (Parts 1, 2 & 3)* then opened at the American Repertory Theater (Diane Paulus, Artistic Director) in Cambridge, Massachusetts, on January 28, 2015. The design and production personnel remained the same. The cast was:

The Musician	Steven Bargonetti

Part 1: A Measure of a Man

The Chorus of Less Than Desirable Slaves:

Leader	Charlie Hudson III
Second	Julian Rozzell Jr.
Third	Tonye Patano
Fourth	Jacob Ming-Trent/Patrena Murray
The Oldest Old Man	Harold Surratt
Hero	Benton Greene
Penny	Jenny Jules
Homer	Sekou Laidlow

Part 2: A Battle in the Wilderness

A Colonel, In the Rebel Army	Ken Marks
Smith, A captive Union soldier	Michael Crane
Hero, The Colonel's slave	Benton Greene

Part 3: The Union of My Confederate Parts

The Runaway Slaves	Charlie Hudson III, Tonye Patano and Julian Rozzell Jr.
Homer	Sekou Laidlow
Penny	Jenny Jules
Odyssey Dog	Jacob Ming-Trent/Patrena Murray
Ulysses	Benton Greene

From the Author's Elements of Style

I'm continuing the use of my slightly unconventional theatrical elements. Here's a road map.

■ *(Rest)*
Take a little time, a pause, a breather; make a transition.

■ A Spell
An elongated and heightened *(Rest)*. Denoted by repetition of figures' names with no dialogue. Has sort of an architectural look:

Hero
Homer
Hero
Homer

This is a place where the figures experience their pure true state. While no action or stage business is necessary, directors should fill this moment as they best see fit.

Production Notes

Staging: Sometimes indicated by "*(Aside)*" but most often not, throughout these plays, I'm widely employing the convention of direct address to the audience. Enjoy.

Music: I've written songs for these plays. We had a musician on stage, visible and "witnessing" and "interacting" with the characters and audience. Most often the musician will sing the songs. In Part 2 (but not in Parts 1 and 3) the characters sing. Lyrics are in the text. Music's in the back of the book. Also, I've written several musical themes which we used as underscoring or punctuation throughout the show. The musical themes are to supplement the dialogue and stage action. Place the songs where indicated. Future publication may provide indication of the musical themes' specific placement, but, in the meantime, imagine them occurring in judicious relationship to their corresponding character or situation.

FATHER COMES HOME FROM THE WARS

Part 1

A Measure of a Man

Characters

The Musician

The Chorus of Less Than Desirable Slaves:
> **Leader**
> **Second**
> **Third**
> **Fourth**

The Oldest Old Man
Hero
Penny
Homer

Dark Is the Night

Dark is the night
Long is the day
Dark is the night
Long is the day
Got time for work
No time to pray.

He's heading out
Or will he stay.

The sun he hides
Don't see his face
The night he crowds
And death don't leave a trace.
Dark is the night
But there's no resting place.

Early Spring, 1862. A slave cabin in the middle of nowhere.
Far West Texas. One hour before dawn.
The Chorus Leader measures the night by holding a hand
up to the sky.
After a moment, the Leader is joined by the Second.

Leader
Leader
Leader

Second
How much time we got?

Leader
How much you want?

Second
Don't be smart.
Hero's gonna be leaving when the sun comes up.
And we gotta know how long we got till he goes.

Leader
Listen to him. Talking like he know.
But we don't know if Hero is going or not.
All we know is the sun's gonna rise, God willing,
But when it comes to Hero,
We gotta wait for his word to know what he's doing.

Second
Me, I'm betting that he's going.

Leader
Are you now?

Second

That's right.

Leader

You're betting that Hero's gonna go to the War?

Second

That's how I'm betting,
Mark it.

Leader

You betting that Hero's going to the War with the Boss-Master?
Working as the Boss-Master's servant-slave?

Second

That's what Hero does here, so that's what he'll do when he
    goes to the War.
His job ain't gonna change just cause he gets to wear a fancy
    uniform.

Leader

You're betting Hero is gonna wait on Boss-Master hand and
    foot?

Second

He waits hand and foot on him now.

Leader

And hold his horse steady for him to climb on top?
And hold his horse again for him to climb on down?
And run behind, carrying all Boss-Master's whatnots on his
    back?
Running behind the Boss-Master and the Boss-Master's
    horse both?
And getting spattered with flecks of dirt
From Boss-Master's horse's hooves?
And getting speckled with bits of bad-smelling release
From that same horse's privates?
And combing down the horse after a long day of fighting?
Scrubbing the horse? Then scrubbing the Boss-Master?

Then putting the Master to bed?
Then combing the Master's coat
And shining his boots.
And Boss-Master, the Colonel, sleeping inside
On a warm cot inside a warm tent.
And Hero, the slave, sleeping outside on the cold hard ground
While the cannons pound and the bullets fly
And the war-wounded holler
Cause their legs and arms are lost, and their hopes are dashed.

Second
Why you got to go on and on about it?

Leader
I'm just making sure you know what you're talking about.

Second
I'm betting Hero's going to the War.

Leader
With the Boss-Master?

Second
Yep.

Leader
As the Boss-Master's slave?

Second
That is what I'm betting. Mark it.

Leader
You got time to change your mind.

Second
I'm not changing my mind.
I'm all decided on it.
I just want to know how long we got until sunrise
Cause that's when I'm gonna collect my share of the winnings.
Sounds like you're betting the other way.

Leader
I am.

Second
You betting that Hero will give up his chance
At greatness to stay here and grub in the dirt?
You betting that, instead of picking a field of battle,
Hero is gonna pick a field of cotton and corn?
That Hero's gonna want a rusty plow for planting
Instead of a shiny medal for bravery?
That he's gonna choose coveralls instead of a uniform?
That he'll be satisfied with having his name only wrote down
In the Boss-Master's counting-book
Instead of getting a chance at getting his name, Hero,
Maybe wrote up in one of them great Histories?
Now you betting Hero's gonna stay home, so you betting for all
      that?

Leader
Mark it.
And I got a good chance at winning too.
As good a chance as him, anyhow. And we'll see soon enough.
We got about an hour before the sun comes up.

Second
Don't look like an hour to me.

Leader
Measure it yourself then.

> Second holds a hand to the sky,
> measuring the night as best he can.

Leader
What you betting?

Second
My spoon.

Leader
I thought you was gonna be buried with that spoon.

Second
I'm betting it but I'm gonna win it back right away
Cause Hero is going to the War.
Mark it!

Leader
I'm betting my shoes.

Second
Both of them?
Oh, winter is gonna be cold for you.
You gonna be shoeless and your feet gonna
Freeze and turn blacker than they are now
And then Missus is gonna chop them off
Cause they'll be frozen. Cause they'll be frost-bit-dead.
And you gonna be walking around like Homer do
But worse:
Homer used to have two feet and now he don't got but one feet.
But Hero, on the other hand, Hero is as he was born:
Big, brave, smart, honest and strong.
The favorite.
He ain't missing nothing.

Leader
Except maybe the War. Snap.

Second
Please.
Anyone else bet?

Leader
Not yet.

Second
Not Penny? Not the Old Man?

Leader
Nobody yet but you and me.

Second
Them two got more sway on Hero than all of us put together.

Leader

If Hero goes he'll be missing them: Penny and the Old Man
   both.

Second

Here are the others
Let's see what they say.

> The other Chorus members enter, ready to place their bets
> and trying their hands at measuring the night.

Third

How much time we got?

Leader

A little less than an hour now.

Second

Some of us are betting that Hero's going to the War.

Leader

And some of us are betting that he'll stay.

Fourth

You might be the best at measuring Night
But that don't mean you the best at measuring Men.

Third

Early risers have their say but we gotta make our own
   choices on this
Each of us gotta make a measure of the man
We gotta choose for ourselves.
(Rest)
I got a brass button
I might be betting that Hero is—
Going to the War.

Fourth

I got a banjo.

Third

Don't bet that.

Fourth
I'm betting it. And maybe I'll bet—
That Hero stays put.

Leader
There is a kind of sport to be had
In the consideration of someone else's fate.

Third
Where's Penny?

Second
Still in her house most likely.

Third
And the Oldest Old Man?

Leader
He woke up early this morning
And he went out in the field to die of shame cause his son
    won't be going.

Second
Or he's dead of fear cause his son will be going.

Fourth
Either way sounds like the Old Man is most likely dead.

Third
It happens. He was pretty much as old as a person should get.

Leader
Woah.

> The Old Man enters.

Chorus
Old Man
Chorus
Old Man

Old Man

Why you all crouching away from me?
It's just the Old Man here.

Leader

Old Man, you dead yet?

Old Man

What kind of foolish question is that?
Good thing you all ain't free.
Good thing they days ain't they own to fill.
Good thing they time is still owned by the Boss-Master,
Cause, if they time ever was they own, mark it:
They'd be filling it all up with foolishness.
Seeing me standing here but thinking me dead.
Goodness, people, I was just out walking, out looking for
    Hero's dog.

Fourth

Hero's dog, the dog called Odd-See.
We all know where Odd-See Dog is at:
Hero's dog is by Hero's side, just like he always is.

Old Man

The dog's run off,
Where he's gone to I don't know.

Third

That's hard to believe.
Hero's dog,
The dog with eyes that go this way and that?

Old Man

Hero's only got one dog.

Second

There must have been something he was chasing.

Old Man

He weren't chasing nothing
Hero kicked that dog.
And then the dog run off.

Third

Old Man, you know Hero don't kick his dog.

Old Man

And Odd-See, his dog, he don't run off neither.
But I'm telling you: both them things happened, mark it.

Leader

Strange news. How will it sway your bets?

Fourth

Strange news on any day but especially today.
Cause of the bond Hero and Odd-See got between them.

Third

The Dog is always by Hero's side.

Second

The Dog lives in Hero's footsteps.

Fourth

All his food comes from Hero's plate.

Leader

And the shade he takes comes from Hero's shadow.

Old Man

And the dog is Hero's good luck charm.
Don't forget about that.

Leader

Now that's just some superstitious nonsense!

Old Man

I'm telling you what I know for true.
Listen up:
Penny, she comes out the door
And when Hero said the dog had run off she got worrisome.
Then, Hero and Homer together, they headed on up to the
    house.

And Penny, left alone, she fell on her knees and prayed a
    quiet prayer:
For Odd-See to come back.
She finished praying on her knees
Then she went praying on her feet.
She walked off, went looking for the dog.
I followed her but I followed slow.
Got tired, headed back, here I am.

Leader
How are you betting, Old Man?

Second
Will Hero stay or head to the War?

Old Man
I ain't ready to reveal my say.

Leader
Still thinking about that dog.

Old Man
It's a consideration.
That dog is Hero's luck.
It's as simple as that.

Third
The sun's coming soon.
And Hero will get himself decided.
Dog or no dog.

Second
Don't make a mountain out of a molehill,

Fourth
Don't make a god out of a dog, Old Man.

Leader
Don't make a snake out of a rope.

Old Man
What I'm telling you is true.
And The Truth will set you free
Even if the Master don't.

Chorus
Old Man
Chorus
Old Man

Old Man
That's Hero coming now.

> Hero enters, coming back from the big House.
> He carries a pair of boots and some worn-out pieces of
> a Confederate Army uniform. The day's events
> and their possibilities have created an air
> of excitement within him. A buoyancy.

Hero
Morning.

All
Morning Hero.

Hero
You all all awake, huh?

Leader
We're waiting on you, Hero.

Hero
Where's my dog?
Why don't he come to greet me?

Old Man
Penny's gone to bring him back.
He's probably out there curled up in a warm spot, sleeping.

Leader
It's still early yet.

Second

Everything with any sense is still asleep.

Hero

Count us among the senseless then. And Boss-Master-Boss
the most senseless of us all. He's been up awake the whole
night working on getting ready and he's still busy at it. I was
trying to decide my mind while I was helping him. And he
knew it too. He kept giving me these looks. But under his
watch ain't no place for this man to think. So I had to excuse
myself and come back here with my mind as unmade as
my bed!
(Rest)
Boss had me and Homer both helping him get dressed.
Homer, after all his years of working outside minding the
mules, he ain't much of a valet, but it turned out all right.
All them uniform whatnots. Boss gave me these remnants to
wear, if I choose to go.

Old Man

Boss' uniform must be a fine thing.

Hero

You'll see it soon enough. All the sashes and belts and
buckles and braids. If I hadn't of known, I'd think Boss-
Master-Boss was decorating himself to join the traveling
circus. He's got this hat with a cream-colored feather that's as
big as a fan, hell, it's bigger than a fan, that feather is twice
the size of Boss-Master's head. I hope the wind don't blow on
it else it'll blow him right off his horse. And his new boots.
To get them on he had to tug and stomp and cuss so much,
Missus comes in running thinking that me and Homer had
attacked Boss-Master. That thought alone is funny. Ha, you
shoulda seen it. Boss-Master, sitting on the bed with Missus
fanning him cause his boots, they fit, but they so new-tight,
you know. And then Homer said, "Lucky you don't got to *walk*
to the War." And that's when Boss-Master laughed.
(Rest)
You all gonna head up to the House to see him head out?

Old Man

He's promised each of us a coin for our trouble so we'll be
there, mark it.

Hero

Maybe you'll be waving goodbye to me too. But maybe not.
(Rest)
Go get some rest, now. Unless night turning into day is
suddenly something special to see.

Leader

Are you going or are you going to stay?

Second

Some of us will bet you'll go.

Fourth

Others'll bet the other way.

Third

What will you decide, Hero?

Old Man

Listen to you all
Feeding on Hero's choice
Like so many buzzards feed.
Cept the carcass ain't one. He's still living.
So let's step away.

Hero

You all clutching ahold of your best treasures.
Odd-See!

Old Man

Plenty of time for him to come home.

Hero

I'm starting to think that dog ain't nothing.
A dog is just a dog.
A dime a dozen.

Old Man
Sit. Rest.
Penny's out looking for him
And we'll sit and watch the dawn come up.
Mark it with us.

> Hero sits with them, measuring the night.

Hero
Chorus
Hero
Chorus

Hero
Why don't my dog come back, do you think?

Old Man
Don't think on it.
Just sit.

Hero
I need peace or quiet at least.
You all go help look for my dog, huh?

Fourth
We jump when you say jump.

Third
We follow you, even if it's just your finger, pointing out the way.

> They go. The Old Man slowly follows them.

Hero
Father.
Stay with me awhile.

Old Man
"Father."
I love it when you call me that.

Hero
If you could have anything you wanted
Could you name it?

Old Man
You granting wishes?

Hero
Would you have your son go to the War or would you have
    him stay?

Old Man
I bet you already know your father's mind.

Hero
Not until I hear it from his mouth.
When I say "War" I try to read your face
But you sense me looking and you turn away.

Old Man
I want you to decide your own self.
Boss-Master ordering you to go to the War with him
And then he tells you that you got a choice in the matter.
The great Boss-Master-Boss gives you your freedom of choice.
Like he figures his freedom of choice is gonna somehow
Take the place of the Rightful Freedom that he's been
    denying you.
Like he figures that his gift, his little crumb of choice,
Will somehow save his soul when the Judgment Day comes.
Me and Penny both agreed to stay clear and let the last word
    on it be up to you.

Hero
Still still still: Do you want me staying home?

Old Man
Yes.

Hero
You want me staying here? Did I hear right?

Old Man
Lemmie shine up your boots for you.
Keep my hands busy.

Old Man

What father in his right mind wants his son going off to the
    War?
I mean, yes, well, maybe *real* fathers.
Lucky men who had their sons shot out into life through
    their own balls
Maybe they figure easy come easy go.
You're my son but as you know
I didn't make you from my spit.
Which makes me, I guess, a fake-father.
But you, Hero, no mistake, you're a real son through and
    through.
No, we don't got the luxury of blood between us,
And your arrival was a happenstance, but all that makes me
Double-bless the day you came here and looked up to me.
And here I am now. Looking up to you.
Oh, I wish I was your real daddy.
Then I could say I knew your Ma.
Cause you got at least half your self from your Ma,
Which means that Woman was a Force Divine.
So if I had known her even for a quick minute: Woah!
I'd still, after all these years, I'd still have that sweet gal on
    my mind.
Lord! I ain't never even met her,
So stop me, son, from crying cause she's gone.

Hero

You can always get me laughing.
Even when things are weighing heavy.

Old Man

I want you to go, son.
There. I said it. I'll tell you true:
I want you to go to the War.

Hero

There's Truth in your voice now.

Old Man

Yes.

Hero

This morning when Boss and me spoke alone together
He promised me:
My Freedom for My Service.

Old Man

Your Freedom?
Your Freedom for your Service?
All the more reason. You'll go now, surely.
Mark it!
I'm readying myself to wave goodbye.

Hero

Not just yet.
He dangled it in front of me. My Freedom.
Like a beautiful carrot.
Like a diamond. And those scraps of uniform and the
    diamond Freedom glittered
As he promised it, asking me to see it, to smell it, touch it,
    try it on for size.
But while I so wanted to I was still thinking on the bald fact
    that in his service
I will be helping out
On the wrong side.
That sticks in my throat and makes it hard to breathe.
The wrong of it.
All those days working in his fields that I thought of killing
    him.
You know those days. I'd come home in a sweat
Not from working but from the rage.
And Penny, understanding but bearing on, like we all do.
I'd be out in those fields behind a plow praying for his
    murder.
How can I last one day on the battlefield
Without doing the same or worse?

Old Man
Kill him and there's no life for you.

Hero
I know.
I won't hurt him. There's my Word.
But can you see Boss-Master and me coming home from the
     War
And him giving me my Freedom like he says he will?

Old Man
It's right for you to wonder.
After the way he promised you your Freedom that first time.
Why do you shiver?

Hero
Just the memory of it.
His First Promise. His very First Promise.

Old Man
That was the only other time he offered you your Freedom.
Unless I'm mistaken.

Hero
Father?

Old Man
Son?

Hero
Nothing.

Old Man
Boss-Master promising in front of everybody and in a loud
     voice:
"I'll give you your Freedom if you cut off Homer's foot,"
And you said, "No!" You bravely refused him.
So Boss threatened you with death
And then the axe came down.
Mark it: Yes, it was horrible

But right now: this Promise is—more promising.
He'll come through this time, son.
Your Service for him and for his Cause will outweigh
    everything
And he'll come through.

Hero
I'll chance it if you feel so sure.
I'll accept his offer. Take him up on his Promise.
And I'll give myself a chance at something great.
And I'll come back here.
And I'll help everybody when I get home.
I'm as good as gone.

Old Man
Put on your uniform.

Hero
It's not a whole uniform.
More like a bunch of scraps.

Old Man
Put it on and wear it.
A man like you can make a wholesome thing out of bits and
    pieces.

        Hero puts on the scraps of his Confederate Army uniform.

Hero
I can see myself, out there.
Guns blazing all around, cannons going off
And the line of endless tents
And the piles of the dead.

Old Man
You won't be one of the dead, son.
You do your service and then
Here you are coming home.
I can see you.
Walking bravely

Hero
And I bow down to you, giving thanks, glad to be back.

Old Man
And your Freedom has been granted
And your dog has been found
And none of your limbs have been lost.

Hero
Mark it.

Old Man
You all dressed?

Hero
Pretty much.

Old Man
Look at you.
How do you look?

Hero
I look all right.

Old Man
Parade around.
Lemmie hear your boots marching in the dirt.

> Hero parades around. He styles and profiles.
> Penny enters. Her presence stops him in his tracks.

Hero
Hold my hand.

Penny
Oooh it's warm.
Look at me, I'm dancing you!

> She moves his arms, making him dance.
> He lifts her up.

Hero
And I'm flying you!

Penny
I'm a bird!

                                    They embrace. It's deep.

Hero
Close your eyes.

Penny
They're closed.

Hero
Kiss?

                                              They kiss.

Hero
Keep them closed. Now look.

Penny
Hero

Hero
I was just trying it out.

Penny
There's planting to be done today
You gonna wear them whatnots and them boots walking
    behind the plow?

Hero
I was just seeing how it felt.

Penny
Feels hot, don't it? If it don't yet it will soon.

Hero
What do you think?

Penny

I think— I think the day's gonna be warm.

And you all dressed up like that and plowing the field—

I think you'll be sweating like the old folks do when they see
a holy miracle.

And I think it'll take you twice as long to get done half as
much

And then everybody would know what I know looking at you
now:

They'd say, "Hero, the man who is practically Penny's
husband,

That man Hero has gone and lost his mind."

Old Man

He's got something to tell you, girl.

If you'd just give him a clearing.

Penny

Tell me what, Hero?

Hero

We've been discussing things.

Penny

I'm ready to add my say.

Old Man

You filled up both my ears already.

Hero

Head to toe, Penny: How do I look?

Penny

That outfit makes you better-looking, Hero, I can't lie.

Hero

Not every man can wear it well.

Hero
Penny

Penny
Let's go inside
And stay in bed all day.

Hero
And miss the War?

Penny
The War is nothing.
You said as much yourself.

Hero
You gone looking for the dog?

Penny
I did.
But I shoulda stayed here and kept an eye on you.

Hero
Odd-See ain't come back with you.

Penny
Even the Old Man can see that.
The way you look would make someone with less conviction
Think they was too late to put the good sense back into your
    head
That seems to have drained clean out from spending time
    with the Old Man.

Old Man
He's made his mind up, woman,
Leave him be.

Penny
His mind don't matter none to me
Cause I know what his heart says.
You don't want to disappoint the Old Man but go on and tell
    him.
He can bear it.

Hero
Hero

Penny
Hero? Go on.

Old Man
Don't keep pestering him.
It's natural for a man to want to go to War
To seek his fortune
To try his hand at grabbing better than what he's got now.

Penny
It's also natural for God to strike dead someone as old as you.
Just cause God ain't yet called his name don't mean He forgot.
I'ma remind Him:
"Lord, You got an old old man down here who You shoulda
    taken a long time ago."

Hero
Don't curse, Penny.
Not on my account.
She didn't mean it, father, so the curse, it didn't get to Heaven.
Girl, we went and talked it through, father and me.
Hear me out, hear?
I'm going.

Penny
But you don't want to go.
You don't want to.
You told me so.
Hero, just this morning.
We woke together.
At the same time. In the same breath like we often do.
You breathed it out and I breathed it in.
And we woke up.
No work to do that early so it wasn't the plow calling.
No rooster up that early and not no sun, Hero.
Just us two.
Everything else was quiet and sleep.
"I got to tell you my mind before the others meddle with me
    and twist me up," you said.
Cause you knew. You knew that that's what they do.

Planting their own seeds into you.
Using you worse than Boss-Master does.
"I'm not going," you said.
"I'll tell the Master so at sunrise," you said.
"Help me keep my secret," you said.
You leaned close to me, my ear to your lips. In the dark it was.
Whispering into my ear.
Putting your words into my head.
"I'm not going to the War," you said.
And, oh, oh, I was afeared for you.
Crossing Boss-Master is a horrible thing.
That's what went through my head.
But also, it was sweet
Even though it was terrifying it was sweet.
That you was not gonna raise a hand against your own cause
That you was not gonna help out Master.
That you would stand up.
That you would stay home.
At least that's what I thought I heard.

Old Man
You woke this morning deciding not to go?

Hero
Hours ago I might of said that.
I might have thought that out loud
And shared it with Penny, sure.

Old Man
You gave her your Word?

Penny
You did.

Hero
I gave you some words in the dark while half sleeping.
What man don't do that?
But now I'm decided.
I'm going, girl.

Penny
You go to the War and for what?

Hero
I got a chance at getting something.

Old Man
He can't explain it, Penny
There is a thing about his call to service
That he needs to keep private until the time is right.
So let's all just accept the hard truth:
Hero has been called to serve and he's leaving.

Penny
Without his dog.

Hero
The dog will be home directly and if he don't come what of it?

Penny
That dog's your luck, Hero.

Old Man
That's just some superstitious nonsense.
It's time for all of us, if we want to grow out of this low place,
To leave behind beliefs like that.
Hero has changed his views and, following his lead,
I've changed my views too.
And so should you.
It's very liberating.

Penny
"Liberating"?

Old Man
"Freeing."
Mark it, woman.

Penny
Boss, he must be promising you something wonderful.
He's promising you your Freedom
Something "Liberating,"
Ain't I right?

(Rest)
I'm right. Mark it. That's what's got your head turned.
At first I thought it was the Old Man's words
But, no, Boss, to sell you on it,
He's promising you your Freedom again, ain't he?
Such a sweet promise!
But how could you even think of saying yes to him
When you know good and well
That his Freedom-promise is only. Ever. Linked.
To something. Bad.

Hero
Quiet!
Quiet please.

Hero
Penny

Penny
Hero?

Hero
Penny?
(Rest)
Daylight will be here shortly.
And here comes everybody.
Coming on back
And they're coming back without my dog.

> The Chorus enters. The Dog is not with them.

Hero
Tell me the news.
Tell me how you found him dead.
Tell me quick.
The creature that brought me nothing but luck
Like other dogs bring their masters bones
You found him dead and his body ripped in pieces.
So horrible you didn't have the heart to bring him back in
    scraps.
Am I right?

Leader
We didn't find nothing.

Second
Not even a hair.

Fourth
We did see his tracks
But they faded.

Third
We called out to him
No answer.

Old Man
So Hero's dog is gone.

Leader
What do you say to that?

Second
Weigh it all careful.

Third
Weigh it in your heart.

Hero
There's still time before the sun is up.
But, hell, I'm all decided.

Leader
Give us a chance to place our bets

Fourth
Cast our votes

Second
Make our sway

Third
Have our say.

Hero
Keep your treasures close. Don't risk losing them.
I'm not going.
There's my mind.
I'll stay.

Leader
It's the wise choice.

Penny
You'll stay?

Second
Hero. Hero.
Think on it.

Old Man
Think on it, son.

Penny
You'll stay?

Hero
I'm staying.
Let the day come.
Let Boss-Master come riding up here wondering where I'm at.
Let him see the scraps of uniform piled on the ground.
Let him see me standing here with you all.
Let him hear me say, "I'll stay."
Let him come. I'll be standing here.
And I dare that man to move me.

Second
But there will be beatings for all of us
When Boss hears what he's decided.

Fourth
The dog running off was smart.
But where will we go to hide?

Third
The whip is a long whip.
Boss' anger will come up

Leader
That's right. He'll beat him hard and
He'll beat us twice as hard.

Second
For his 10 lashes we'll get 20.

Third
For his 20 we'll get 40.

Fourth
For his 50 we'll get 100.

Hero
I won't go. I can't. My heart's been set against it from the start.

Chorus
Hero
Chorus
Hero

(Rest)

Old Man
So you'll have to harm yourself in some way.
To take the edge off Boss' anger.

Leader
A finger or two cut and bleeding

Third
He'll be wounded.

Second
Missing a part of himself, maybe.

Penny

We'll all say it was an accident.

Old Man

In the heat of getting ready
And in the darkness

Fourth

A knife fell in the wrong place

Third

Didn't Boss hear your screams we'll ask him?

Hero

He'll be up at the House, wondering where I'm at.

Leader

And when he comes riding up to see for himself

Second

He'll see Hero. Not standing in defiance,

Fourth

But lying wounded on the ground.

Old Man

It'll be all right.

Hero

I'll harm myself in some bloody way.

Old Man

You'll ease up the harm Boss wants to do to us.

Hero

I'll do it.

Penny

He'll hurt himself to keep us safe.

Hero
You'll take my foot.

Penny
Your foot?!

Hero
Do like I say.
You'll take my foot.
That seems fair.

Penny
No.

Old Man
We'll do it or get beaten dead for his defiance.
One of you will whet the knife.
And Penny, you'll hold him while I make the cut.

> Leader whets the knife. Hero puts his foot
> on a rock to be cut off.

Third
It's still dark out
There's still time to reconsider
Hero you were born perfect and lived your whole life whole
Is that to end here? Is that to end now
In front of a ruined cabin with an old knife?

Hero
Harm won't come to no one but me.

Fourth
Won't some angel come
And hold back the hand?
Where is the big voice
Telling us that all this is just some kind of test
To see if we were willing to follow the path.
Where is the path? Where is the path?!
The path, it isn't marked.

Won't some spirit come down
Some angel, some light, some mercy?

Leader
The sun is coming by my measure, mark it.
But the day is getting darker seems to me.
Homer is coming. Maybe we should wait for him.
He might have an idea for this.

Second
Before we worried about our bets
That we'd lose what we laid down.
We were only thinking about winning something
But now, there's Hero, ready to lose a part of himself
To save us from a greater harm that's surely coming.

Old Man
Hold still, son
I've got a sure hand
And a kind heart.

As the Old Man raises the knife, Homer enters.

Chorus
Old Man
Hero
Penny
Chorus

Homer
Whatchu all up to?

Hero
You got eyes.
You can see.

Homer
So go ahead and do it if you're gonna do it.
Old Man you feel your mark all right?

Old Man
I do.

Homer
You got him held good, Penny?

Penny
I do.

Homer
You decided that you're staying, Hero?

Hero
I'm decided.

Chorus
We'll swear to it.

Homer
Cause that's the only reason you all would be organized like
    this, mark it.
You're gonna spare us Boss-Master's full wrath and fury.

Hero
I hope to.

Homer
You all don't just stand around looking.
Somebody get something to stanch the blood.
Get some rags, plenty of rags.
Get a bucket.
Cause there's gonna be plenty of blood
Remember how it was with me, Hero?
But with you it's not gonna be like it was with me:
Hero won't be having his blood to spilling on the ground
It's hard for a man to see that
Harder than losing his foot I think
To see his blood spilling out on the ground
To see the earth
Drink it up

Greedily drinking, greedy,
And nothing growing back.
And the foot cut off
And left on a pole to rot
Least that's how Boss-Master did mine.
Remember?
Left it on a pole right over there
Dared any of us to take it down.
Hero took it down
And got whipped.
Penny took it down.
And got whipped.
So it stayed up there and rotted.
Hero,
All that talking you was doing with Boss-Master about how
You going to the War with him and you ain't going after all.

Hero
Too many signs pointing to stay.
Penny's words, the dog not here, my own heart.

Old Man
And my own heart
Frail as it is
Can't no longer raise this knife
Take it Hero
If you need your foot cut off
Then you do it your own self.

Homer
Go on, then.

Hero raises the knife but does not bring it down.

Homer
Yeah.
I'm not the oldest here,
But, Hero, since we come up together
I've known you longest
And I figure maybe, in some respects I know you best.

Hero
You do.

Homer
His knife ain't coming down cause his mind ain't decided.

Hero
My mind's made up.

Homer
Then let the knife come down.
When has one of us ever had a choice except for you, Hero?
You'll always be lucky.
Go on
Let it fall.

> Hero cannot maim himself.

Penny
Give it to me then
I'll do it.

> Penny tries in vain to take the knife from him.

Leader
You're right, he's not decided yet.

Second
If you were betting, Homer, how would you bet?

Fourth
There's so much riding on it.

Third
And poor as we are
Each of us would surely love to take home the winnings.

Homer
I'm not betting either way.

Hero
I thank you.
Everybody has a stake in what I do but you.

Homer
Go to the War
Stay Home.
Those your choices?

Leader
Those are his choices.

Penny
The knife.

Hero
Take it.

Hero gives the knife to Penny.

Homer
I say don't.

Hero
Don't?

All except Hero and Penny
Don't?

Penny
Don't what.

Homer
Don't.

Penny
He's got to do one or the other, Homer.
Don't make his mind more tangled up than it is already.

Homer
He shouldn't do neither.

Old Man

Who needs your raggedy opinion anyhow?
The sun is coming
And Hero's going
And that's his father's word.

Penny

The sun is coming
And Hero's staying
And that's the word of the gal he loves best.

Homer

Mark it, people
Anybody who wants to win the bet
Mark it:
See how they each pulling on his coat
Penny, she's got her woman's love and she's pulling him to stay
Old Man, he's got his father's love and he's pulling him away.
Penny, she's got a knife and if Hero stays that'll hurt for sure
Old Man, he's got the War waiting, and that'll hurt more than
    100 knives.
Go to the War or stay at Home?

Hero

Stop making a game of it.

Homer

Ain't no game, Hero.
Cause you shouldn't be doing neither.
Cause you shouldn't stoop
To do neither
Cause both choices, Hero,
To stay here and work the field
To go there and fight in the field
Both choices are
Nothing more than the same coin
Flipped over and over
Two sides of the same coin
And the coin ain't even in your pocket.

Hero
I'll give you that.

Leader
But what else is there for one like us?

Second
We gotta take what we've been handed.

Penny
Fieldwork is honest work.

Old Man
But Boss-Master is promising Hero his Freedom.

Leader
His Freedom!

Old Man
His Freedom for his Service.

Second
Promising Freedom?

Homer
That man will never free you. Ever.
You're waiting for him to give you Freedom
When you should take it.
Yeah.
I been thinking on it.
Boss-Master will be sitting up there, expecting Hero, but
   Hero, see,
Hero will be long-run-off and gone!
"Hero has misplaced himself," Boss-Master will say.
Hells yeah.
I can tell you how to go.
All that mapping I used to do
I still got it all in my head.
I'll tell it to you, Hero.
Mark it, now's the time.

Start running and you'll be free so quick
The War will still be raging and
Master will be promising Freedom to the next fool
Fool enough to believe it.
And you,
You'll have your Freedom already.
Taken.
Taken for yourself
It'll be completely yours.

Leader
This idea is a third way
Something to consider.

Old Man
What do you say, son?

Penny
I'm ready to stand with whatever you decide.

Hero
I ain't never been one to run from nothing.

Homer
Your father ran away.

Hero
And look what it got him
Hanging from a tree.

Homer
That won't be you.

Hero
How you know?

Homer
So you won't run away cause you're scared?

Hero
I'm not scared.

Fourth
Hero's father was wild but Hero is mild?

Hero
I'm not scared.

Old Man
What is it then?

Hero
He promised me.
He gave me his Word.
I want him to make good on what he promised.

Homer
You're a fool.

Hero
Heavy words deserve heavy hands.

Homer
Don't beat me, Hero.
It won't look right for you
The one who cut off my foot
To beat me down.

Hero
You shouldn't have tried to run off.
I told you so back then
And you got caught
But I told you
If you just worked hard
Everything would be all right
Years later, here we all are
Working hard and things are all right, more or less,
Aren't they?
Except you don't got your foot.
If you hadn't tried to run off you could of still had your foot
    today.
And I wouldn't have to bear the burden of
Being the one who was forced to maim you.

Homer
Back then when I run off
We were supposed to head out together.
But then I guess you went and changed your mind.
Boss-Master and his like finding me,
Surrounding me, dragging me back here.
And you cutting off my foot.

Penny
You can't blame Hero for that.

Hero
He threatened me with death
Put a gun to my head
And that's what got the axe to swing.

Second
We were all there.
We all saw it.

Leader
Any one of us would have done the same.
There's harm in it but no blame.

Old Man
My son was only doing his best
Caught as we all are between a rock and a hard place.

Homer
But still the axe came down, didn't it.

Hero
It did.

Penny
And you'll leave it at that. Please?
We've all heard enough.

Homer
So after what he made you do to me
How can you ever believe Boss-Master
When he promises you the moon and stars?

Hero

Cause I ain't like you.
I ain't some wild man who will
Break away from good common sense and
Go running. Go running here go running there
Go running who knows wherever.
No real map no real nothing and getting no real freedom that
   way.
Grabbing, taking, snatching, begging, borrowing, stealing?
My Freedom's gonna be free of that.
Cause who would I be when I'm free that way?
Something stolen. A Stolen-Freedom?
That ain't me.

Homer

Seems like
After all the wrong Boss has done
You're no better than a dog.
Or worse than your own dog
Who at least had the sense to run off
When his Master kicked.
You're a dog what gets fed scraps from the table
A dog what gets kicked then stays around.
A dog what follows his Master no questions asked.
You're like that Hero.

Hero

I should of cut off your other foot.
I should of cut off your head.

Penny

Peace.

Third

Be kind. Be kind. Make your words gentle.
Counsel him on whether he should go or stay.
But don't make him feel wrong wanting Freedom his way.

Leader

The sun is coming and Hero is heading one way or another.

Second

We want the bonds between you to be good.

Fourth

No matter what's decided.

Old Man

Even though you all are owned by another man
Your words are your bond.
They're part of your record.
Words and deeds both.

Homer
Homer

Homer

Did you all know
That it was Hero who lead them to me.
Did you all know that it was Hero who told where Homer
    had run off to.
I was gone but nobody knew which way I'd went.

Old Man

That's a lie
A lie to make confusion.

Fourth

We can't believe it.

Leader

Set the story right, Hero.

Hero

I don't recall the circumstances of that day
With this day here crowding in my head
And all you all crowding around me.

Second

Just tell us how it really went.

Third
We don't need a lie about you hanging in the air.

Homer
I'll tell you how it went.
Boss told me so.
He was drinking just now he was drinking trying to get his
    courage together
Cause he's going to the War,
And he starts talking to me as if I'm you.
I dunno, Hero, do we look alike?
Cause he confused me for you.
But you had left to come back here, and it was only me
    alone helping him get ready:
And him drunk and thinking I'm you,
Talking, making it be certain-known that, unlike any
    promise made before,
This time, his Promise of Freedom would be a sure thing.
Not like the time before.
And here, ok, I thought he was gonna talk about the
    Freedom for the foot
(And how it didn't work out too good)
But he brought up something else:
A time before that:
The First Promise he called it:
The day he promised you your Freedom
In exchange for *you* telling *him* which way *I'd* run off to.
And how you went and told him.
How you gave me away.
How you pointed them to me.
And still he didn't free you.
"But it wont be like that this time," he said.
"This time I'll come through," he said.
You gave me away.
He told me so.
Then drunk Boss-Master-Boss realizes
That he's telling Homer instead of Hero.
And he went all quiet.
Not another word.

Leader
Freedom in exchange for giving Homer away?
And you said yes.

Old Man
Lies.
Homer is nothing but envy and bile.

Second
Freedom in exchange for breaking the bond of trust.
And you said yes.

Old Man
Lies.

Hero
Believe it.
It's true.
Boss gave me a hundred reasons why I should tell.

Old Man
Why are you lying on yourself, son?

Penny
It's true.
Years ago Hero told me
And I've held it in our confidence.
Like he told me to.

Third
Freedom for giving Homer away.

Hero
Boss told me—
He talked up close inside my ear and he said—
He said—
And thought, I thought—
I don't know what I thought.

Homer
When Boss said jump you jumped, that's all.
You told on me to him.

I told on you to Them.
That makes it even.

Old Man
All we've got is the trust between us.
(Rest)
I can't call you son anymore.

Leader
And we can't call you Hero.

Penny
That's still his name.

Third
Maybe we won't call him anything at all.

The sun rises.

Chorus
Penny
Hero
Homer
Chorus

Second
The sun is up.

Hero
And my need to leave is clear.
Not run off, Homer,
Although I can see there's a value in it,
But it's not my road.
I'll go trot behind the Master.
The non-Hero that I am.
Odd-See!

Fourth
He calls his dog
His dog that brings him luck.

Hero
Odd-See!

Second
Does the dog hear him?

Hero
Odd-See dog!

Leader
The dog no longer knows his voice.

Third
The dog no longer knows his name.

                                    The Dog does not return.

Hero
The sun is up
And Boss-Master waits
I'll go.

Homer
Boss will give each of us a coin for waving them goodbye
And a whipping if we don't.

Penny
I'll go and wave goodbye
Then I'll be here. Right here.
I'll wait for you.

Leader
Let's all go to see him go.
A broken man on a dark dark day.

                    Hero exits followed by Penny, Homer and the Chorus.
                            The Old Man rises to go but then sits.

Old Man
To have a son leave home is no small thing

But losing a son before he leaves
That's more than an old man can bear.
I'll sit and wait for his return.
He promised he'd come home.
With luck it won't be long.

End of Play

He's Leaving

Oh, he's leaving
He's leaving you all
At the break of day
He's leaving
All you all
At the break of day
Don't know yet where he's heading
But he knows he cannot stay.

And the gal he loves
She's making Perfume
Perfume when she walks
Yeah, the gal he loves she's making
Perfume when she walks
I wouldn't never cross her
She will cut you like a hawk.

Farther and farther,
He'll be going
Farther and farther down the *way*
Farther and farther
Gone on down the way
Lord, give him good company, cause
He won't be home again today.

FATHER COMES HOME FROM THE WARS

Part 2

A Battle in the Wilderness

Characters

The Musician

A Colonel, In the Rebel Army
Smith, A captive Union soldier
Hero, The Colonel's slave

Late Summer, 1862. Around twelve noon.
A wooded area in the South.
Pretty much in the middle of nowhere.
The Colonel sings "Passing the Time,"
and modestly accompanies himself on a banjo.
His Union prisoner, Smith, is captive in
a makeshift wooden cage.

Colonel

I've sat on a mountain I've sat on a hill
I love God and Country, I pay all my bills.
I'm a pretty good husband, though don't ask my wife
If she catches me here, I'll pay with my life.

They made me a Colonel, got me a white horse
Upstanding, distinguished, with servants of course.
The Grey and the Blue and the dead and the brave
All hoping to get back home one of these days.

Yes, I've told you once and I'll tell you again
I've drunk all your beer and I've drunk all your gin
I've had all your whiskey and I've downed all your wine
Just sitting here lonesome and passing the time.

The Colonel stops singing.

Colonel

You're not singing. I taught you the tune. Taught you the
words. You don't recall them?

Smith

I recall the words fine. It's hot.

Cannon fire in the distance.
The Colonel directs Smith to move the cage to a shady spot.
After Smith completes this task he's allowed to remain outside.
Cannon fire in the distance.
The singing contunues:

Colonel

This war, it's a fierce one there's battles there's cannons
Cold food and cold tents and a fear of the famine.
They might catch you or shoot you or give you the pox
And the way you come home might just be in a box.

Sing with me.

We got a handful of brave ones and a handful of cowards
We got a Yankee, smelling rotten, and needing a shower.
We won't die in these woods, we'll surely find our way back
And give old Mr. Lincoln one hell of a whack.

Colonel and Smith

I've told you once and I'll tell you again
I've drunk all your beer and I've drunk all your gin
I've had all your whiskey and I've downed all your wine
Just sitting here lonesome and passing the time.

Smith

I've wandered the mountains and I've wandered the hills
Now I hear the big guns and the sound gives me chills.
I'm being held prisoner by a drunken dumb Jeb
When I get my freedom I'll cut off his head.*

Colonel

Changing the words is not polite. Dirty-wounded-flea-bitten-
pus-oozing Yankee. I should have left you in the field for
dead. Your own Regiment left you. I should have left you
too. Let you die there. Instead I carried you along with me.
Into this shady grove.

---

* The original lyrics, as taught to Smith by the Colonel are: "I'm being
held prisoner / My leg's bleeding red! / I'm lucky he found me. I'd been
left for dead."

Smith
Where I'll bleed to death.

Colonel
You were shot in the leg not in the head. And it's nicely
bandaged. You'll live.

Cannon fire in the distance.

Colonel
Those cannons can't be more than 10 miles away. I'll be able
to deliver us back to the Regiment before nightfall. What a
fool I was for straggling off. My fit of pique. Then we got lost.
Horse died. Bad luck. Had to walk. But then I find you, left
for dead, a Union Captain, a prize. When I get back and show
them my prisoner! My captive Union Captain—well, there
will be a hell for me to pay, but when I come back leading you
by the scruff of the neck I'll get a wonderful thanks for it.

Smith
I'm just a Captain.

Colonel
You're an officer in the Union Army. You're a white man.
Lucky you're not a Union nigger. If you were, I'd be
obligated to shoot you on the spot. (An obligation that's not
in any book, not written down, history would find it barbaric,
so we keep it unspoken we don't speak of it we just shoot on
sight.) Lucky for him that he's worth something more than
money. Yes and you're worth something alive even though
you are just a Captain—

Smith
—Just a Captain.
(Rest)
If I was a Major, you'd get more than a thanks, you'd
probably get a medal for me. That's how the Union would
work it anyhow.

Colonel
We reward the same way.

Smith

What if I was a Colonel. Or a General.

Colonel

If you were a General I would get a promotion.

Smith

If you'd caught a General you'd get the moon and they'd cover you over with stars and you'd get a golden goblet from General Robert Edward Lee's own house, a golden goblet for you and your wife both.

Colonel

One for me and one for my wife, hand-delivered by General Lee's best nigger.

Smith

Yes. Maybe. And you'd get plenty of money. And you'd get more land. If I was a General they'd make you the richest man in the state.

Colonel

They'd give me all the land I wanted and without a bald spot on it. Every inch of it, just as green as you please. And 10 teams of mules that don't kick too much.

Smith

You'd get 10 teams of mules that don't kick at all.

Colonel

And I'd get a mistress. Who is kind. And a little wild. If you were a General I'd get mistress.

Smith

But I'm just a Captain.

Colonel

Yes. That's a shame.

Smith
Ours or yours, you think?

Colonel
Ours. Certainly ours.

Smith
You sure?

Colonel
I'm a Colonel. I'm sure.
(Rest)
You're a Captain serving in the 1st Kansas Colored Infantry.
What's it like leading them?

Smith
It's like leading anyone else, I suppose.

Colonel
You've had experience leading whites?

Smith
No.

Colonel
Then you can only suppose that your experience is similar.
Your Coloreds, left you for dead in the field.

Smith
I suppose I looked dead. The men in my command are good
men. Hardworking. Brave. They do what I tell them.

Colonel
They do what you tell them to do, they're hardworking,
they're brave, have you ever wanted to own them?

Smith
No.

Colonel

I'm not asking you to imagine owning a whole field-full but just one have you ever had the desire to own. Own. Own one just one of them?

Smith

No.

Colonel

Not a one?

Smith

No.

Colonel
Colonel

Colonel

I had a son. He died. At an early age. You remind me of him. The way he would disobey me.

Cannon fire in the distance.

Colonel

Drink with me at least. I don't have much left but I'm courteous enough to share it.

Smith

I couldn't.

Colonel

I insist. As your captor I insist.

Smith

I'm a sober man.

Colonel

A sober man and a slaveless man. Living your life with neither bottle nor slave. When you get back home and I'm guessing you will, they may have to remove your leg but you'll live. You'll get married, I'm guessing you're not already and you'll have your children, I'm guessing you don't have any yet, not even a bastard, your kind don't have bastards, everything your kind do is legitimate, you'll live out your life, with one leg, though, don't forget the one-legged part of it, and on your dying bed surrounded by loved ones, you'll have two private thoughts just before the great blanket covers your head just before the Great Master puts his big hand over your face. First: I should have indulged in spirits, hit the bottle just a little and your second dying-bed thought would be: I should have owned one of them. A darkie. Just one. Just for a day. Just for the feel of it. Because there's nothing like it.

Smith
How many do you own?

Colonel
Me? A hundred. And would I add to that number? No. Because there's no need to. "Reason not the need"! Oh, hell yes, I most certainly would add to my hundred slaves because it's the mark of a fine man to own them and one can't have too many.

Smith
Huh.
(Rest)
We captured a Jeb awhile back. He didn't own any slaves but he'd been promised 10 for his service. "10 is a good number," he kept saying. He didn't have a dollar to his name. He signed up for the war in another man's place, see, there was a rich man, who had been called up to serve, and, the rich man didn't want to come to the War so he got this poor fellah to come in his stead. Said he'd give him 10 slaves for his trouble when he got home. The fellah was pretty excited about the prospect. "10 is a good number," he kept saying. He had the promise-paper in his pocket and he'd show it to our Colonel every chance he got.

Colonel
You told that story already.

Smith

Did I?

Colonel

You've got a fever.

Smith

A bit. Hell, I'm alright. I'm fine. The sun makes it hot.

Colonel

Drink. Water.

Smith

Thank you.
(Rest)
"10s a good number," our prisoner kept saying.

Colonel

10 times 10 is a better number. You're wondering what it would be like.

Smith

Not at all. I'm a Yankee through and through. Even if I took off my blue coat I'd still be a Yankee. Even if you made me swear to the Rebel Cause I'd still be full of my Yankee blood and my Yankee ways and notions. Even if I came down here to live even if I lived down here for a hundred years and had a hundred slaves I'd still be a Yankee.

Colonel

Underneath your blue coat you and me are more alike than different. And I know you are looking at me and you're thinking that it's only a matter of time before we see things your way and we are looking at you and thinking the same thing.

Smith

We don't want to change you, we just want to whup you.

Colonel

You won't. Ever. Because deep down you think like we think. Agree with me.

Smith
Smith

Colonel
You're from one of those aristocratic families, aren't you?
One of those wealthy elite groups in that New York City or
Philadelphia? Your daddy's a rich man? He is, isn't he? And
you were brought up with a silver spoon in your mouth. Well,
I was brought up with a wooden spoon in mine. Self-made.
But not you, am I right? Tell me. That would be something,
wouldn't it? We'd get your likeness in the newspapers. We'd
ask for a ransom. You'd be a prize prisoner. A real prize.

Smith
I'm not.

Cannons fire in the distance.

Smith
(Rest)
You aren't scared I'll run off?

Colonel
You can't hardly walk.

Smith
I'm a wiley Yankee. You'd best keep your eye on me.

Colonel
And I'm a "dumb drunk Jeb" with a loaded pistol.

Smith
You best keep me close. Closer than did your man-servant.
He's run off, isn't he? I didn't want to mention it, but you
sent him to collect wood and water and that was a good hour
ago. He's run off.

Colonel
He's not run off.

Smith

I don't see him around here.

Colonel

He's collecting wood and water. I "collected" the rabbits.
He's collecting the wood and the water.

Smith

He's run off. You got to keep them close or they'll run off.

Colonel

Your niggers ever run off?

Smith

I don't got none.

Colonel

Your soldiers. In your command.

Smith

We got deserters and stragglers just like everybody else but
it's different. Even if they do leave the Regiment they're not
escaping like yours did. Maybe you should go look for him.
It was more than an hour ago. You come walking in here and
him following behind with those rabbits and then you telling
him "go fetch wood and water," and off he went. I bet when
you get reunited back with your Regiment, your General's
gonna be looking at you. And he'll be looking at me. You'll
lead me in by the scruff of the neck, just like you plan to,
and your General will be reaching for a medal to give you.
Shoot, he'll be taking a medal off his own coat to give you
that's how impressed he'll be with your prisoner. And then!
He'll notice. That your valet is no longer with you. Hero,
you call him. Hero is nowhere to be seen. Hero has misplaced
himself. Oh dear. Oh, he'll still give you the medal all right
but all the fellahs will be snickering at you behind your back.

Colonel

Get back in your pen.

Smith

Walking around, getting fresh air made my tongue wag like a dog's backside.

> The Colonel considers shooting, but instead he kicks Smith in his wounded leg.

Colonel

You're worth more alive than you are dead. Plus one doesn't want to waste the ammunition.

> Smith retreats to his cage and the Colonel locks him in.

Colonel

You might have commanded them but I own them. And because I own them I have an understanding of them that you don't have and never will. Hero knows his worth to the penny, and, well, the poor thing is honest. Meaning he won't run off not now not ever. He told me one day: "Master," he said, "running off, well, that would be the same as stealing," he said.

Smith

He came to the War with you. He came willingly?

Colonel

I asked him to join me and he did so without a second's thought. To get him on board I had to sweeten the pot. I promised him his Freedom.

Smith

And you'll keep your word?

Colonel

Things these days have grown so very complicated.

Smith

You don't intend to keep your word to him.

Colonel

I didn't say that.

Smith

So if he serves you well, you will keep your promise, yes or no?

Colonel

Lucky we found this span of trees. The shade they provide.
(Rest)
Footsteps approaching. Hero!

Hero

Yes, sir, I'm coming directly.

> Hero enters, loaded down with firewood
> and carrying a bucket of water.

Colonel

He's returned. What took you so damn long?

Hero

I was getting a look at the armies coming this way.

Colonel

Any scouting that needs scouting I'll do it.

Hero

Where should I lay it down?

Colonel

Just there. Get the fire going so we can eat.

Hero

Fire's gonna tell them where we are.

Colonel

And we'll be reunited all the sooner.

> Hero makes the fire.
> The meat has already been skinned and skewered.

Hero

I seen the Yankees coming. They got a big bunch marching
and they're steady on the move. Rebels coming too but not
as strong and not as fast and not as many.

Smith
How close?

Hero
Smith

Colonel
Both sound like they're about 10 miles off.

Hero
That's what it looks like to me. Both armies headed this way.
One coming from one way, one coming from the other.

Colonel
Get the supper going.

Hero lays the skinned rabbits on the fire.

Hero
There ain't plenty of wood out there like you would think.
You'd think, us being in the middle of the woods, that there
would be plenty of wood. But there ain't.

Colonel
You saw them. With your own eyes.

Hero
I did. You handed me your binoculars so I figured I should
use them.

Colonel
I'll take them back now.

Hero
Yankees are marching strong but they're way further off.
From what I seen, the Rebels are closer to where we're at.

Smith
But the Yankees are marching stronger?

Hero
Smith

Colonel
I'll eat something then I'll go and see for myself.

Hero
You'll catch us up to the Regiment before the day is out,
Colonel, just like you say. I know they'll reach us. Or you'll
reach them. The world ain't that big a place.
(Rest)
I got the water too. Like you said. Filled the bucket and
didn't spill but a little. And all the wood's good and dry.

> Hero's got the fire going and the meat cooking.

Colonel
I'll see to the supper. You'll see to my boots, huh?

> Hero helps the Colonel pull off his boots.
> The Colonel minds the fire as Hero shines the boots.

Colonel
You might as well shine up the Yankee's.

Smith
No need for that.

Colonel
I want you looking good when I hand you over so hand him
your shoes.

Smith
I'll wipe them down myself.

Colonel
Don't deny me the opportunity of extending my hospitality.

Hero
I don't mind none.

Smith hands Hero his boots. Hero then takes off his own boots and works on polishing all three pair.

Colonel
He's a good worker. You gotta give him that. And trustworthy. I told you he didn't run off. Captain Smith, if you'd of had money you would have wagered that he'd cut and run and you would have wagered incorrectly.

Smith
Did you run off, Hero?

Hero
Smith

Colonel
Go ahead, answer the Yankee. Even though your Master believes he's one of the devil's minion, you can still talk to him, Hero, go ahead.

Hero
No, sir, I didn't run off.

Smith
Did you want to?

Hero
I'm not from around here.

Smith
That's a good answer.

Colonel
Captain, how much is Hero worth? In dollars and cents.

Smith
Your dollars or ours?

Colonel
Yours.

Smith
I wouldn't know.

Colonel
Hazard a guess.

Smith
I wouldn't.

Colonel
Amuse me.

Smith
No thank you.

Colonel
Play along.

Smith
I said no.

Colonel
He's not much fun, is he, Hero?

Hero
He seems alright.

Colonel
But he's ignorant of your worth. So we'll school him. Just for sport. Let's say the Captain guessed 500.

Smith
I didn't.

Colonel
But we'll say you did. Captain Smith guessed 500 because he doesn't know any better. Major Lewison, Hero, with our Regiment, he says he's got two negras about your size and age and he paid about 500 a piece for them. So common knowledge would say 500.

Smith

And common sense would say—

Hero

Keep quiet. Common sense would say keep quiet.

Colonel

Major Lewison would price you at 500. And Lieutenant Beauchamp—

Hero

The pretty one who's always combing his hair?

Colonel

Always talking about his father's thousand acres and thousand slaves. He would set your price lower. 400. But which price is correct? Before the sale was made, a prospective buyer would need to hear a report of your conduct. Hero's a good worker, we've all seen that. He's of the trustworthy type, meaning that he don't run off or stir up trouble. To sum up the report of his conduct, we'll say that Hero minds his Master. That adds an extra hundred or two. If we agreed on the base price as the average of the two prices then we'd be at a price of around 650.

Smith

Consider me adequately schooled.

Colonel

But we're just getting started.
(Rest)
Now that you've heard of his character it's time to discover if your prospect's got skills. You've got skills don't you, Hero?

Hero

Farmhand. Valet.

Colonel

And as his Master I can vouch for his high competence in both. Now we're at about 700. Skills in blacksmithing?

Hero

No. You know that already, Colonel. But I could learn it if I had to.

Colonel

Blacksmiths go for as much as 2 thousand.

Smith

Very informative. And that's enough for me.

Colonel

Where are we, Hero?

Hero

Colonel?

Colonel

Are we in the North or the South?

Hero

We're lost.

Colonel

We are lost in the South. Trying to pass the time until our Regiment advances to such a proximity so as we might strike out on foot with the confidence that we will be successful in our efforts to rejoin ourselves to Ourselves. And while we wait. In the heat. We indulge in conversation. Small talk some might call it. But the Yankee, he declines.

(Rest)

> He sings a bit more from "Passing the Time":

Colonel

I've buried my father, I've buried my son
Won't bury myself though, when my life is done.

I tell you what, Captain Smith.

> The Colonel invites Smith to exit the cage.

Colonel

Play along with us and, if you can, using the information provided, if you can determine Hero's original worth, that is, the price he was when he came to me, then he'll be yours.

Hero

Just like that.

Smith

You'd have your freedom in a heartbeat.

Hero

Just like that?

Colonel

Just like that. Now, just so it's all above board, Hero knows his purchase price so we can't accuse the Colonel of dishonesty should the Captain guess correctly. All right with Smith?

Smith

All right with Hero?

Hero

Alright.

Colonel

We'll continue with the inspection.

Smith

Go.

Colonel

Hardworking, trustworthy. Smart but he'll behave. No skills in reading and writing.

Hero
Colonel

Smith

Is that true?

Colonel

No more than what I showed him and he and I have agreed
that it will always be our secret, how and what he's learned.

Hero

Yes, sir.

Smith

Thereby proving he can keep a secret. I'd say that's worth
100 more. Should I name my price now?

Colonel

Not yet not yet. We've made an inspection of his moral
character now we will make an inspection of his person. His
physical person. Stand.

> Hero stands up.

Colonel

You got most all your teeth?

Hero

I believe so.

Colonel

But you should never take them at their word.

Smith

You said he was trustworthy but you don't trust him?

Colonel

Open up your mouth.

> Hero opens his mouth. The Colonel takes a quick glance.

Colonel

Let the Yankee have a look.

> Hero moves to where Smith can see inside his mouth.

Smith
Thank you.

Colonel
He's got more teeth than me.

Smith
So you know two things: he's got his teeth and, as you said before, he's not given to lying.

Colonel
And how much is he worth given his skills, his good character and having most all his teeth?

Smith
The grand total?

Colonel
Yes now's the time let's hear it.

Hero
Smith

Colonel
Don't look at Hero. He's not going to tell you with a look. Eyes to the ground, Hero. Now, how much?

Smith
I'll say a thousand.

Colonel
You're very good.

Smith
Am I right?

Colonel
Hero how much did I pay for you? Look at the Captain wringing his hands in anticipation or worry. How much, Hero? You know. I know you know. You sneaked a look in my ledger book one day and I knew you did but I didn't whip you for it. You saw how much I paid. How much was it?

Smith
A thousand?

Hero
800.

Colonel
Oh. My apologies, Captain.

Hero
I might be worth a thousand now.

Colonel
You came to me 10 years ago. When you were a much younger man. Your price would be lower now.

Hero
But I've learned things. Skills add to value.

Colonel
I see your point. If a man wanted to buy you from me today, how much should I ask for do you think?

Hero
Hero

Smith
Leave him be. Leave us both be.

Colonel
You want me to sit here by myself. In the middle of the wilderness. When we're with the Regiment, and when we're at home, Hero, is positively charming. But here, I have to prod him to participate. That does not bode well. It makes me feel—unsettled. Unsettled inside. It makes me forget the promise I made to you, Hero.

Hero
To figure out my price today, you got to consider whether or—

Colonel
Heat or cold, rain or shine, you work just as hard.

Hero
Whether or not you'll win the War, I meant. The price I'd fetch today would have something to do with that. That's the way I see it.

Smith
Good thinking.

Colonel
Hero

Colonel
Stand up Hero and undo yourself. We need to finish the inspection.

                                        Hero is thinking: Nope.

Colonel
Undo yourself.
(Rest)
First, we will do a visual inspection and then, we'll do more than just look. As my own father used to say, "Never trust the eye in these 'private' matters. Only trust what your hand will tell you."
(Rest)
Undo yourself, Hero.

Hero
Hero

                              Hero is thinking: No fucking way.

Smith
Stop.

Colonel
Undo yourself I said.

Smith
Stop.

Colonel
Hero
Smith
Colonel

Colonel
Alright. For his sake. We wouldn't want the Yankee to die of fright.

> The Colonel approaches Hero and, quickly raising his riding crop, he strikes Hero across the face.

Colonel
Captain, oh, Captain, how ill-equipped you are for life in the modern world. You're a dying breed.

Smith
You don't know anything about us.

Colonel
"Us"?

Smith
Us Yankees. Us from the North.

Colonel
Forgive me, Hero for striking you.
(Rest)
It's been a long day.
(Rest)
A toast to you. A toast to you. Honest, trustworthy, never seen him touch spirits or tobacco, knows his numbers and letters could learn additional trades if necessary, and he's musical. Taught me what little song I manage. A toast to you a toast to you. I'm singing your praises. Here I am, actually singing your praises. Sing with me? The one about toiling?

Cannons fire in the distance.
The Colonel begins singing "This Bright Wilderness."
Hero eventually joins in.

Colonel

In the midst of this most fearful day
Let us count our many blessings
In the midst of this bright wilderness
Let me see the light I know.

Hero

In the darkest of the darkest night
There is still a day that will come all right
God is in his Heaven up above up above
While we toil bravely down below.

Cannons fire.

Colonel

Take out my plume. Fix it on my hat.

Hero takes out a slender box. He removes a large white plume.
Suitable for framing.
Hero affixes the plume on the Colonel's hat. Splendid.

Colonel

Yankee. What do you think?

Smith

You're making an easy target out of yourself.

Colonel

Perhaps. I used to wear it all the time. Then only on Sundays
and when I had to review the troops. Now I mostly just carry
it around in a box. Hero made the box. These days I only
wear it in the privacy of my tent. Or in places like this.
The wilderness.
(Rest)
Hero, you have many extraordinary qualities. Were my son
living I would want him to be, well—

Hero

Should I put the feather away?

Colonel

Not just yet.

Cannons fire in the distance.

Colonel

The Yankee thinks I'm a bad person. A bad man. That I'm in
the wrong. That I engage, all of us like me, that we engage in
bad acts. Constantly. He forgets that I've promised you your
Freedom for your Service, isn't that right?

Hero

You gave your Word on it.

Colonel

So I'm not all bad. What will you do once you're free?

(Rest)

Hero

I couldn't say.

Colonel

I know what I would do. I would be sorry to see you go.
I would be. And Missus. She would stand on the porch
crying and I would put a brave face on it while you went off
down the road, heading who knows where to do who knows
what, she'd be crying and I'd be standing there wearing my
brave face. Once you rounded the bend, out of sight, gone
never to return, we'd have supper. Missus crying in her soup
and me, making too much conversation. Then would come
night fall and we'd be getting ready for bed, Missus would
have the bed covers pulled up over her head and I would be
sitting on the bed, unable to lie down. Cause I'd be feeling
like my good life had left me. Just like I felt when my son
died but worse, cause you wouldn't be dead, Hero, you'd just
be gone. And I'd weep.

The Colonel breaks down crying. Real tears.

Cannons in the distance.

The Colonel regains his composure.

Colonel

I am grateful every day that God made me white. As a white I stand on the summit and all the other colors reside beneath me, down below. For me, no matter how much money I've got or don't got, if my farm is failing or my horse is dead, if my woman is sour or my child has passed on, I can at least rest in the grace that God made me white. And I don't ever have to fight the Battle of Darkness. What difficulties I may encounter will at least never be those. Life might bring me low but not that low. And I know that I will be received in most any quarter. And if the Lord should choose to further advance my economics, then I will be received in all the great houses. Not so with the lower ones. The lower ones will always be lowly. No matter how high they climb. There is a kind of comfort in that. And I take that comfort. For no matter how low I fall, and no matter how thoroughly I fail, I will always be white.

Hero
Smith
Colonel

Colonel

Let's put the plume away.

Hero removes the plume and places it in the box.

Smith

Colonel if you were put up on the auction block, what kind of price would you bring, do you think?

Colonel

That's a Yankee question.

Smith

Clearly as it came out of a Yankee's mouth.

Colonel
I'd bring a better price than my negra, I can tell you that.

Smith
How come?

Colonel
I won't stoop to answer.

Hero
It's an honest question.

Colonel
Hero

(Rest)

Colonel
Things that are worth more bring more money.

Smith
And you're worth more.

Colonel
Stand up.

Smith
You're worth more than him. You're worth more than a Colored? Are you worth more than me?

Colonel
Take off his coat and tie his hands. I'm going to shoot you dead. Prepare yourself.

> Hero begins to remove Smith's coat and secure his hands.
> Smith is wearing two Union coats. One underneath the other.

Hero
Two coats. How come?

Smith
One coat belonged to a dear friend who died.

Colonel
Shot by us, most likely.

Smith
He was a Private. He died of fever. I wear his coat to keep me warm.

> The Colonel aims his gun at Smith who briefly bows his head in prayer. Then:

Colonel
Ready! Aim! Fire!

> But the gun only clicks and the Colonel laughs.

Colonel
Hero, did you see his eyes? They were as big as two saucer plates. Lock him back up.

> Hero returns Smith to his cage. He briefly examines both coats.

Smith
I appreciate you sparing my life. Even though I'm bleeding to death most likely.

Colonel
I'll get a commendation for you.

Smith
And now you've also got my thanks. And I'm glad I could give you a laugh.

Colonel
Give him back his coats.

> Hero returns the coats. He watches as Smith puts them back on.
> Cannons fire in the nearer distance.

Colonel
You said they were about 10 miles off?

Hero
The Yankees. Most likely closer now.

Colonel
And our Regiment?

Hero
Closer than that. But not as many.

Colonel
Hero

Colonel
I'll go and get a look. You'll watch over the camp.

Hero
Alright.

Colonel
If you all win, their Freedom will come surely. And then what?

Cannons in the nearer distance.

Colonel
Wish me luck.

Hero
Alright, Boss. Good luck to you.

The Colonel heads out.
Hero stands at full attention until the Colonel is out of sight.
Then he stands "at ease."

Hero
Hero

Hero
Smith

(Rest)

Smith
You can have a seat.

Hero
I don't need your permission.

> Still keeping a wary eye on the prisoner, Hero tidies up camp.
> Cannons in the distance.

Smith
The cannons. Is it us or them, do you think?

Hero
I don't think nothing, Boss.

Smith
I'm not Boss to you.

Hero
Alright.

Smith
You're Hero? My name's Smith.

> Smith extends his hand.

Hero
All right.
(Rest)
We don't need to shake hands.

Smith
It's courtesy when two men say hello.

Hero
You're a Yankee prisoner in a wooden cage.

Smith
Yes I am.

Hero
You might die before the night's out.

Smith
I might.

Hero
Smith

Hero
You got children?

Smith
Not as yet. You?

Hero
No. Not yet.

Smith
If I had children I may not have signed up. Children make a man cautious.

Hero
Children make a man brave, seems to me.

Smith
As long as I can get back home with both my arms still working good.

Hero
I was thinking I'd want to have my legs. I pray for God to keep my legs on me.

Smith
I pray for arms. Especially with my leg shot up. I'll get home and hug my mother close. I'd need arms for that. I used to pray for legs too but there's probably a limit to what you can get so I'll be satisfied with just my arms. One leg's not so bad. And they got those wheeled chairs that would help me get around.

Hero

You're right. There probably is a limit. So I'd want my legs. Although Colonel says that the Book says that He is a limitless God, yeah, it still don't hurt none to be on the safe side and not ask for too much.

Smith

I raise my hat to your legs.

Hero

To your arms.

> Raising their caps, they salute each other.

Hero

You know I seen the Colonel sleep in the full sun. But me, I'm a working man. Can't sleep with the sun directly overhead. You rest. Go head. I'm keeping watch.

Smith

Shouldn't sleep. Can't.

> Cannons in the distance.

Hero

Guess the Union's got good food, warm beds, pretty women visiting.

Smith

We sleep on the ground and eat bad.

Hero

What about that Mr. Grant?

Smith

The General?

Hero

He lives in a big house?

Smith
He might but I've never seen it.

Hero
The Colonel says that General Lee's got a fine house. How many slaves does General Grant got?

Smith
I don't think he's got any.

Hero
He's a rich man, though.

Smith
Most likely. What I know surely is he's smart. Crafty. Thinks circles around everybody. He once snuck into a Rebel camp and got to know all their ways and snuck out again and they didn't even know he'd been there. And he sneaks up on his own men all the time. That's the key to his strategy.

Hero
Sneaking up on his own men?

Smith
He puts an old coat over his General's gold braid. Hides his medals from sight. Puts on an old cap and maybe some dirt on his face. And he walks around camp or he's sitting by the fire listening to the common soldier in conversation. Getting to know the tenor and the pulse.

Hero
So he can lead them better.

Smith
That's right.

Hero
And they never figure it's him?

Smith

Sometimes, after he's gone. They'll take a count and wonder who the stranger was.

Hero

And they bust a gut when word gets around that General Ulysses Grant done made a courtesy call. Like a fox in a hen house.

Smith

Except he's working to save the hens.

Hero

You ain't General Ulysses are you?

Smith

I'm sure not. Although I do appreciate the question.

Hero

Cause that would be something, wouldn't it? When we catch back up with them—

Smith

Or when they catch back up with us—

Hero

To have a prize prisoner. But you're just a Captain. With a Private's coat underneath.

Smith

What rank are you?

Hero

They don't give me no rank. I'm just the Colonel's Hero. I'll get my reward if I make it through.
(Rest)
What about that fellah you all caught, the one who says he's getting the ten slaves for his service?

Smith

He died.

Hero

Huh.

Smith

The Colonel, he really owns 100 people?

Hero

More like 10. He's only got 10 of us. He works us like 100, but we're only 10. He likes to talk big.
(Rest)
You talk like a Captain. So I guess you must be one.

Smith
Hero

Cannons in the distance.

Hero

2 coats you got. And that Captain's coat you're wearing over top is too big. The Private's coat is the one that fits you.
(Rest)
You a Private?

Smith

—. Yes.

Hero

Huh.

Smith

It was my Captain who died. On the battlefield. When it got dark it got cold. I put his coat on over mine to keep warm.

Hero

You're a Private serving in the 1st Kansas Colored Infantry.

Smith

That's right.

Hero
The 1st Kansas Coloreds they got Coloreds as Privates.

Smith
That's right.

Hero
Smith
Hero

Hero
You a Colored man?

Smith
Yes.

Hero *(Aside)*
I'll be damned. I've seen some before that don't look it. He's one of them. Well, I'll be damned.

Smith
Does your Colonel know?

Hero
Hell no.

> Smith again extends his hand for a handshake.
> A more possible moment now.

Hero
What's it like, carrying a gun, having a Regiment?

Smith
It's an honor. A big feeling that's hard to put into words.

Hero
You can stand up straight when you think about it.

Smith
That's exactly right.

Hero

You think you all will beat the Jebs?

Smith

God willing. And then the whole world will change. You'll be able to have your own farm. Or you'll move North. Or anything you want.

Hero

You're really Colored?

Smith

I could pass. Yeah. Get myself more money, better rank. Plenty like me who can, they do it. But that's not me.

> Smith shows Hero a mark on his forearm.

Smith

My old Master, he branded each and every one of us.

Hero

To tell the world you belonged to him.

Smith

In case we ran off.

> Hero releases Smith from the cage.

Hero

Did you?

Smith

Never.

Hero

Thought about it.

Smith

Sure. Plenty.

Hero

Boss-Master branded us too. Right here. That and lots of other things.
(Rest)
What kind of price you fetch these days?

Smith

I got my freedom handed to me when the Master died. But, if I remember right, I was worth about the same as you.

Hero

And Freedom might be coming.

Smith

It'll come. One way or another, it'll come.

Hero

How much you think we're gonna be worth when Freedom comes? What kind of price we gonna fetch then?

Smith

We won't have a price. Just like they don't. That'll be the beauty of it.

Hero

Where's the beauty in not being worth nothing?

Smith

We won't be able to be moved around, beaten, bought or sold, forced to work and make men rich while we stay poor.

Hero

Most soldiers they're poor, Colored and White both.

Smith

There's more to Freedom than I can explain, but believe me it's like living in Glory.

Hero
Who will I belong to?

Smith
You'll belong to yourself.

Hero
So—when a Patroller comes up to me, when I'm walking
down the road to work or to what-have-you and a Patroller
comes up to me and says, "Whose nigger are you, Nigger?"
I'm gonna say, "I belong to myself"? Today I can say,
"I belong to the Colonel."

> Imagining being confronted by a Patroller, Hero holds up his hands.
> Reminiscent of: "Hands up! Don't shoot!"

Hero
"I belong to the Colonel," I says now. That's how come they
don't beat me. But when Freedom comes and they stop me
and ask and I say, "I'm my own. I'm on my own and I own
my ownself," you think they'll leave me be?

Smith
I don't know.

Hero
Seems like the worth of a Colored man, once he's made Free,
is less than his worth when he's a slave.

Smith
Is that how come you don't run off?

Hero
Maybe. I'm worth something so me running off would be like
stealing.

Smith
Seems to me you got a right to steal yourself.

Hero
Maybe. Maybe not.

Smith

How about you try on my coat. Go ahead. Try it on.

Hero

A Union Army coat in the rank of Captain.

Smith

Try it on. I won't tell no one you wore it. Go ahead.

> After a quick glance ensuring that the coast is clear, Hero hurriedly
> tries on Smith's extra coat.

Smith

Looks good on you.

Hero

Feels good. Don't know if it's the Captain part or the Union part. Probably some of both.
(Rest)
You know what I call the Colonel behind his back? I call him "Peacock."

Smith

"Colonel Peacock"?

Hero

No, just "Peacock." Him and that fool bird-wing feather in his cap that he loves so much. "Peacock."
(Rest)
Sometimes I think there's a broke part of me inside. Snapped in two. Huh.
(Rest)
The Colonel, he says, "Get over here, Hero, and do this and that." And I say, "Yes, sir," out loud but to myself I say, "Sure thing, Peacock, sure thing, Peacock." Sometimes he wonders why I'm smiling and that's how come.

Smith

"Peacock." That's good. Huh. Hero's a good name.

Hero

Colonel named me that. Master before him only called me Joe. Who named you Smith?

Smith

It was my father's name. If you could name yourself anything what would you be?

Hero
Hero

(Rest)

Hero

That's a big question. I don't rightly know.

Smith

Both of us. Satisfied with the names they gave. Huh. This world is such a mess. How's a Colored gonna make his way? Seems like we either get sold off by somebody or sell out our ownselves. You could be bought and sold and so could I.

Hero

That'll end with Freedom.

Smith

But what if it don't somehow? Sometimes I get the feeling that the heart of the thing won't change easy or quick. Cause of the way we were bought and brought over here in the first place. Maybe even with Freedom, that mark, huh, that mark of the marketplace, it will always be on us. And so maybe we will always be twisting and turning ourselves into something that is going to bring the best price. That's the way we were born into this, so is it always gonna be like that for us, slavery or not? Freedom or not? Are we ever going to get us a better place in the marketplace?

Hero

You're talking like you wanna burn something down.

Smith

I'm just saying: if you say you're broke, I say you're double-broke—snapped in two without a penny to your name and hoping someone'll pay more than 800 dollars for you, but goddamnit, God willing, some day we'll have a place besides just the auction block. And maybe that starts by stealing yourself. Steeling yourself, making yourself like metal on the inside. Maybe it'll get better from there. But, I don't know.

Cannons sound in the near distance.

Hero

Footsteps. Someone's coming. Take back your coat.

Hero returns the coat. Smith returns to the cage.
As someone approaches the camp Hero draws his knife.
Hero rushes toward the approaching figure, knife drawn.

Colonel

Hero!

Hero

Yes?

Colonel

It's only me.

Hero

Colonel.

Colonel

Knife drawn. Put it away. God. I should have called out to you as I came up but I didn't think—

Hero

The sun's in my eyes. And the heat.

Colonel

Put your knife away.

Colonel
Hero

Hero puts away his knife.

Smith
You saw them. Coming this way.

Colonel
Hero, pack up the camp.

Hero begins to pack up the camp.

Colonel
If we move quickly we'll be able to catch up to our Regiment.
They're not as great in number as they were when we left
them. They'll welcome us. We'll have to move quickly.

Smith
The Union Army's closer, aren't they?

The Colonel rapidly removes Smith from his cage,
tying a thick rope around his neck.

Colonel
Hero. Take hold of this rope and lead the Yankee along.
With his leg he won't be able to move as fast as you so carry
him if you have to. I'll head out and find us the quickest
way. And if he tries to run off, you call out to me and I'll
shoot him dead, you hear?

Hero
He won't run. I'll see to it.

Colonel
I trust you will.

Colonel
Hero
Smith
Colonel

Hero
We'll follow behind.

Colonel
God Bless.

> The Colonel heads out quickly.
> They watch the Colonel move out of sight.
> Hero holds tightly to the rope fastened securely
> around Smith's neck.

Hero
Smith
Hero
Smith

Smith
Let's go. We don't want to fall too far behind him.

Hero
Smith

(Rest)

> Hero unties the rope from Smith's neck.

Hero
I don't know if I'm qualified to give freedom to another man
seeing as how I'm not a free man myself but I give it to you
just the same. God willing I'll make up for a horrible wrong
I did.

Smith
What kind of wrong?

Hero
No matter. If you're lucky you could move down the hill
some, lay low for a spell, then join back up with your fellahs.

Smith
How you gonna explain me being gone?

Hero
I'll think of something. Not to worry.

Smith
Hero

> Smith quickly removes his Private's uniform coat.

Smith
You're coming with me. Put it on.

> Hero just holds the coat.

Smith
Raise your right hand and solemnly swear.

Hero
I swear.

Smith
Well done. You're a Union Soldier now. A Private in the 1st
Kansas Coloreds. Come on.

> Smith moves to leave. Hero doesn't follow.

Hero
Hero

Smith
Come on!

> Cannon fire in the very near distance. Rumble in the earth,
> fire and danger in the air.

Smith
Come on!

> Smith tries to pull Hero along. No luck.

Smith
Hero
Smith
Hero

> A parting embrace.
> Smith heads northward, toward the safety
> of the oncoming Union Army.
> It's doubtful that he'll make it.

Hero
Hero
Hero

> Hero removes his Confederate uniform coat.
> He puts on the Union coat.

Hero
Hero
Hero

> Then he replaces the grey army coat, pulling it over the blue one.
> And Hero heads southward, taking the path the Colonel took, back
> toward the heart of the Rebel Army stronghold.

This Bright Wilderness (Reprise)

In the midst of this most fearful day
Let us count our many blessings
In the midst of this bright wilderness
Let me see a light I know.

In the darkest of the darkest night
There is still a day that comes all right:

God is in His Heaven
Up above up above
While we toil
Bravely down below.

When the Road is long and the Eye is weak
Let us hope the Heart is merry.
Let us keep on keeping on, you know.
Let us cherish all we carry.

When the thick is thin and the plenty ends
It will be as it has always been:

God is in His Heaven
Up above up above
While we toil
Bravely down below.

God is in His Heaven
Up above up above
While we toil
Bravely down below.

End of Play

FATHER COMES HOME FROM THE WARS

Part 3

The Union of My Confederate Parts

Characters

The Musician

The Runaway Slaves
Homer
Penny
Odyssey Dog
Ulysses

Misplaced Myself

They be looking high and low
They be looking in the trees
They be searching on the rivers
They be questioning the bees.

I'm long gone
I ain't sitting on your shelf
I have misplaced myself
I have misplaced myself.

I ain't working in your field
I ain't minding in your store
I ain't churning up your butter
You don't matter anymore.

I'm long gone
I've skipped town with all your wealth
I have misplaced myself
I have misplaced myself.

I ain't leaving you no trail
I done went and broke my chain
You got everything to lose
I've got everything to gain.

I'm long gone
I ain't sitting on your shelf
I have misplaced myself
I have misplaced myself.

Fall, 1863. Far West Texas. A slave cabin in the middle of nowhere.
Late in the afternoon, about an hour before sunset.
The Runaway Slaves huddle together on the porch.

Third Runaway
Do you think she'll dream again tonight?

Second Runaway
What difference does it make? Who is she to us?

First Runaway
She fed us. 3 good meals. No questions asked.

Second Runaway
No questions cause it's dangerous for them to know our
business. Runaways like we are. The less they know the less
they can be made to tell.

First Runaway
Penny: she's a good cook. And Homer: "the man who's got
the land written down in his mind," he's out in the field right
now. While we sit here, he's stealing from his Missus' crops
so we'll have food when we head out.

Second Runaway
We don't need to get too deep with them is all I mean. The
little we already know of them is more than plenty. As things
stand, it's safer that way.

First Runaway
Ok ok.

Third Runaway

Still and all: I can wonder. And I wonder if she'll dream again tonight. I wonder what she dreams of.

First Runaway

Her husband, Hero, that's clear enough cause she calls out his name.

Third Runaway

But what of him? Must be horrible. The way she wakes up screaming. And running from the cabin. And Homer hurrying out behind her. And the way he has to hold her close. And cover up her mouth.

Second Runaway

Lucky for us, by nightfall we'll be gone on our way, so at midnight, if she does dream and scream, we'll be too far gone to hear her.

Third Runaway

And so, what difference does it make you're thinking?
(Rest)
We came here figuring Homer would run off with us right away but he said no. Why you think that is?

First Runaway

Because of his foot. He's lost his foot and his confidence.

Third Runaway

It ain't that. It's Penny, she's rooted here. And Homer is rooted to her.

First Runaway

Which makes her something to us.

Third Runaway

Tru dat.

Second Runaway

Then I say we go on without him. We've come this far. We can find our way to freedom on our own all right.

Third Runaway
We can kinda-sorta.

First Runaway
We can maybe. Not.

Second Runaway
Our luck's dried up then. It's hopeless. I'll go hang myself from the nearest tree. I'll go cut my own throat. I'll go jump in the river and drown.

Third Runaway
Please. We got a little more than an hour before it's dark enough to jet. That's time enough to get Homer to change his mind.

Second Runaway
Good luck with that.

First Runaway
We'll work on him together. Mercy. Here he comes.

> Homer enters from the fields, carrying a small sack of
> harvested vegetables. He also carries a newly found stick.

The Runaway Slaves
Third: "Before I'll be a slave, I'll be buried in my grave."
Second: True dat.
First: True dat, right, Homer?

Homer
I couldn't say for sure. Truth is a funny thing, you know?

The Runaway Slaves
Third: The Truth will set you free.
Second: True dat.
First: True dat for sure.

Homer
What's for sure is you been running and now you resting. Here's food for your journey. No one saw me and if they did they just thought I was working. Where you all from exactly?

The Runaway Slaves
The Runaway Slaves

Homer
What's the use getting friendly if you'll be gone by nightfall?
Yeah, ok. Keep me at arm's length and I'll give a good wave
goodbye when you go.

The Runaway Slaves
First: I ran from a place east of here.
Second: I ran from a place further south.
Third: And I ran from a place further south than that.
First: We met up on the road.
Second: And now we're running together.
Third: Running buddies you could say.

Homer
And you're waiting for night before you move on. The moon
was gone last night. You shoulda left then.

The Runaway Slaves
First: We were waiting for you.
Second: Still are.
Third: Say you'll come with.

> Using the stick, Homer practices writing in the dirt.

First Runaway
We're leaving out tonight.

Homer
It'll still be safe to travel. The moon will be just a sliver.

First Runaway
Our best chance is if you come with us.

Homer
Things are different now. Changed.

The Runaway Slaves

First: You're still Homer.

Second: And we're still here waiting.

Third: You know how to read the land and sky.
You can read the weather and the birds.

First: We've got papers.

Second: We made them ourselves.

Third: Some for you too.

First: Just say the word.

Second: Slavery, in a way, it don't got nothing to do with the
Master.

Third: Remember who you are. Here's your chance to be true.

First: True dat.

Second: You'll go tonight with us.

First: Whatchu say, huh?

Third: Whatchu say?

Homer

You can read and write your letters good. I thank you for
teaching me this much. How's this look?

The Runaway Slaves

First, Second and Third: Looks like you're learning.

Third: There's more reading and writing where we're going.

First: Come with us and we'll make it.

Second: Won't be easy—

First: But we'll make it. With you we'll make it all the way.

Third: "Ain't nobody gonna turn me around."

Homer

Don't get ahead of yourselves.
(Rest)
Once I thought I was gonna make it all the way. Just like
you. And this porch here is as far as Homer got. There's
worse things, though. The last time I ran they cut off my foot.

The Runaway Slaves

Third: But you can still walk, can't you?

Second: And you can walk good.

First: You will walk away tonight with us.

Homer
I don't think so.

The Runaway Slaves
Third: Now's your chance.
Second: You got runaway blood.
First: Run away and follow that.

Homer
Not so fast now.
(Rest)
You know sometimes I sit here thinking about my foot and
how I'll grow me another one. Lizards can do that, why not
me? We don't work that way. Ok. Things could be worse.
I got a good place here. But no foot. I got Penny by my side.
But no foot. Penny dreams of Hero. I dream of my foot. Now
some letters. Still no foot. There's worse things.

First Runaway
There's better.

Homer
Such as?

The Runaway Slaves
Freedom.

Homer
I don't know.

First Runaway
Then stay.

Third Runaway
And rot.

Homer
I can't leave Penny.

Third Runaway
Because of love?

Homer
Because of work.

First and Second Runaway
Please.

Homer
Wouldn't be fair to leave her here all alone with the Missus.

Third Runaway
Hero might be coming home soon, the way she dreams of him, wouldn't you say? Or is that just the way I'm reading it?

Homer
She dreams about him in a way that makes me think that he's close by. But dead or living, I don't know.

Second Runaway
If he's living, and if he should come home, better for you to be long gone, don't you think?

Homer
I've made my peace with Hero. What he owes me I can't never get back. And what do I want to take the place of my foot? Not this place, no. But, huh, a new place could be just the thing. To run and to make it to Freedom. To do the thing I always said I'd do. That would show him. I'd show him by being long gone. That'd be something. It'd be funny. I'd be laughing. And Hero, oh he just might laugh. In the even-ing-out of things, he just might see the humor in it.

Third Runaway
So you'll go?

Homer
(Rest)
I'll go. Lord help me I will.

The Runaway Slaves
Good.

Third Runaway
And Penny?

First Runaway
Maybe she'll come too.

Third Runaway
It would be a joy to you if she did.

Second Runaway
And happy men got a spring in they step.

Third Runaway
You wouldn't be looking back over your shoulder and thinking of her.

First Runaway
And that would be a help as we move forward.

Homer
Penny will stay. We're foolish thinking that her mind will change. What that gal does is her own doing. Not mine. And don't you worry, I won't be waving goodbye any longer than necessary.
(Rest)
Penny, she don't got eyes for me. Not ears neither. All she sees and hears is Hero coming down the road, even though he ain't coming. She's a true wife to Hero if there ever was. And it's not like she's on my mind no way no how. Hell, I'm going with you. That's for sure. Leave all this behind.

Homer continues practicing his letters in the dirt.

The Runaway Slaves
Third: I made a choice one morning
Between the ones I loved
And the thing I loved more than them.
Second: They say you shouldn't love things
More than people.
They say that things,
Things come and go.

First: But people, people, they come and go too.

Third: Too true that.

Second: Too true that.

Third: I loved my mother. Left her behind.

First: I loved my brother. He died.

Second: I loved my sister. She was afraid of the dark.

First: I loved Master, in a way, and he, he left his mark.
He did right by law but wrong by me.

Third: Penny, she does right by law, but wrong by you.

Second: Strange thing to love someone who does you wrong.
Even if they do you wrong by doing right.

First: You don't care for her, so you say, but "Penny."

Third: The only word you wanna write.
"Penny" in the dirt. "Penny."

Second: Over and over and over.

> Homer glances down the road then back to his writing.

Homer

It's just a word. One of many. She's just a gal. Nothing more than that. She ain't mine.

The Runaway Slaves

Even so.

Homer

Even so nothing. She ain't tied to me. My foot weren't tied to me. And I ain't tied to this place. So I'm going. To my Freedom. True dat.

> Penny comes in carrying a bag of seeds.

Penny

How long have you been looking down the road for me, Homer?

Homer

Not at all. We've been busy.

Penny

Tell the truth. Scratching in the dirt with that stick.

Homer

I was worried. Patrollers on the road. Sundown will be here soon.

Penny

There's still plenty of daylight and folks know I work for Missus. I can share some of this with you all. Missus won't miss a few handfuls. And don't worry, I was up at the house all day but I didn't do or say nothing to give you away.

The Runaway Slaves

First: We're grateful.
Second: We thank you.
Third: When a good man thinks of love he thinks of you.

Homer

Bad news? You got trouble on your mind. I can see.

Penny

What's that scratching say?

Homer

It says everything.

Penny

"Everything." Is that how you write it? Looks pretty.

Homer
Penny

Homer

Kiss?

Penny

Homer.

Homer

No harm in asking.

Penny

Because you like the sound of no.

Homer

There's a yes in that no. Curled up inside somewhere. Kiss.

Penny

Tell me: whatcha think of my dreams? I dreamed true about Hero's dog: that his dog returned to him in the War. And months later Missus heard the same news in a letter from her Colonel.

Homer

That was something. You could make money telling folks if it's gonna rain.

Penny

Don't make fun.

Homer

I'm not.

The Runaway Slaves

First: A skill like yours is a kind of reading.
Second: You're reading a page that ain't wrote yet.
Third: You got value that would be better spent in a better place.

Penny

You think?
(Rest)
Up at the house, just now, there was a letter on the table. Opened up already. And Missus sitting in the kitchen. Fighting back tears. I asked if the letter'd brought news. She looked up to the sky, like she was praying, but no words.

Homer

Bad news. What'd she tell you.

Penny

At first all she gave me was a look. And this bag of seeds. Nothing else. She told me to get on back here and I went on. I was a good span away when she comes running up after me. When I seen her running I was wanting to run too, but

not towards her—you know, she was yelling so I thought she
was in one of her whipping moods, so my feet stayed rooted
to the spot, figuring if there was blows coming I'd take them
then and there cause me running would just fan her fire, you
know. She come up to me, face dripping with sweat, hair
all which-away. Bending over double to catch her breath.
Finally she can speak. The words come quick.

Third Runaway
What's she say?

Penny
Mumbling something about a Proclamation or some such.

Homer
Proclamation?

First Runaway
What about?

Penny
She was rambling. I couldn't make head or tail of it.
"War's still going on," she says. "Proclamation," she says.
"Freedom," she says.

The Runaway Slaves and Homer
"Freedom"?

Penny
Then, the clearest part, hollered out, "The Colonel, he's dead,"
she says. "He's free cause he's dead."

The Runaway Slaves
Second: Dead.
First: Dead in the dirt.
Third: And your Hero?

Homer
What of Hero?

Penny

"And that Hero of yours, he's dead too," she says. Hero dead too.

Homer

Dead.

The Runaway Slaves

Hero dead.

Penny

And then—she hugs me.
(Rest)
She was just that sad.

> Homer moves to console Penny, but she stops him,
> keeping him at arm's length.

Penny

Let me alone with it. Let me alone with it.
(Rest)
There's worse things. I seen it coming: he's dead. There's worse things.

Homer

Leave with us tonight.

Penny

Leave? Here? With Hero practically home?

Homer

He's dead.

Penny

Oh. With you saying it somehow I believe it. I couldn't believe it coming from her mouth but I can believe it coming from yours. Just let me alone with it. Can't cry. Not yet. Can't yell. Not today. She can cry. Not me. Gotta save my strength. But for what. Do something. Walk. Work. Move. Flee. Run. Don't think I can outrun it, though. Still can't cry yet. Can't yell yet. Will some day. Not today.

Homer

We're heading out tonight. You'll come with us.

(Rest)

I'm leaving with them tonight. You'll come with me. We'll be together.

Penny

On the road, hiding from shadows. Cold, hungry, and the Patrollers. What, you want them to catch you and cut off your other foot, or worse?

Homer

I'll make sure you're safe. These people are good people. Smart. I know the land. And I'll make sure you don't go hungry and at night, at night, I'll, I'll—and I—I Love You.

Penny
Homer

(Rest)

Penny

What's that say again?

Homer

P-E-N-N-Y. It says "Penny."

Penny

You're not right somehow. You're a good man, Homer. What you want with a gal like me, I don't know. A married-gal now a widow-gal. You head out with them and get North and get yourself a good job and a nice gal. I still see him so you best start looking at something else.

Homer

You won't be sad forever. Maybe some day, a kiss—

Penny

No.

Homer
You're sad now.

Penny
I'll get back to work. He promised he'd come home. And when he comes I'll bury him, if they bring him. I'm ready to move on. But not with them. And not with you.

The Runaway Slaves
First: We'll be leaving soon.
Second: And we appreciate your kindness.
Third: Homer will guide us and you'll give him your blessing when he goes.

Homer
I'd like more than a blessing. How about a kiss? A kiss goodbye, right?

Penny
Homer.

Homer *(Aside)*
We spent time together. How she can lie down with me but not ever kiss me, I don't know.

Penny *(Aside)*
I laid down with him because there was room in my bed. It was empty. But my heart, it's full. No room in there for nothing else.

Homer
You're fearful, I'm brave: no matter. I got one foot you got two: no matter.
(Rest)
There's big things and then there's bigger things that small them up, you know? Over where I came from, the sea was so big. But the sky smalled it up. My younger days got smalled up by my years. My one foot gets smalled up by everything. You want to wait, but he's dead and you're scared. Going could small that up.

(Rest)
No better time to leave than tonight. And there's nothing left
to do but go.

Penny
No.

Homer
Then just a kiss, then. A goodbye kiss if not for nothing else.

Penny gently kisses Homer.
And again. It's love.

Penny
Homer

The Runaway Slaves
Second: Tied to this place.
First: But the bond is coming loose.
Loose loose.
Second: Another bond comes up
To take its place.
First: A bond to something better.
Third: The weight that keeps her here
The weight to the dead
To the past
That pulls her
From underneath the ground
It breaks
With tears
That will come some day
But not tonight
Tonight
She'll free herself.
She can't help it.

Penny
I'll go. With you and them. We'll all leave tonight together.

Homer
I'll get everything ready. I was just going to go with nothing,
but now, with you, you'll need things.

Penny
My Hero's dead. I'm gone.

The Runaway Slaves
First: With you, we'll be a joyful group.
Second: We'll travel with speed.
Third: We just might make Freedom by morning.
First: You got word that your Hero's dead.
Third: You've made a wise choice.

Penny
But should I wait? Just to make sure. Cause look, even now,
coming this way, someone—or something.

The Runaway Slaves
Hero?

Penny
No, too small for a man, probably just a wild thing.

First Runaway
A wild thing called Freedom is calling.
Tonight is your best chance
And with nothing to wait for here
Any longer, Penny,
You owe it to you
And to those who will come through after you.
The ones who will come after
The one you're carrying now.

Penny
How did you know? I'm not far gone.

Third Runaway
We can read the signs, Penny.
The look in your eye
The lift in your step
The new one will come

You'll piece together the broken parts.
You two will make it new.
True dat.

Penny
My child. Me and Homer's.

Second Runaway
You will come with us tonight and wake up in Ohio
Or California even
"Soon to be living in a brand-new state."
Where the sun is always shining.

Penny
Help me bear it. Help me bear it. Help me bear it.

Third Runaway
We'll shoulder the burden.

Penny
I'm going. True dat. And I'm glad.

> An actor as Odyssey Dog comes in. He sees Penny
> and runs around and around her, gently calling her name.

Odyssey Dog
Penny! Penny penny penny penny penny.

> Penny embraces him. He giggles and wiggles
> then boldly licks her on the face.
> Hearing the excitement, Homer comes outside.

Penny
Homer! Oddsee Dog is home!

Homer
Look at you, boy! Look at you!

Odyssey Dog
Oddsee's home! Oddsee's home! Oddsee's home!

Penny
You sure are home, aren't you?

Odyssey Dog
It's true, Penny, it's true. I ran off, nobody could find me.
Hero left. I found Hero. But Hero isn't Hero anymore. Yep
I'm home. Yep. Yep. Yep I got news. I got news I got news
lots to tell happy I'm home good to see you. So many dead.
The Old Man dead. The others dead or sold off. That's sad.
Whodat what's that smell? Strangers. New folks. Runaways.
Runaways. Woah. Shhh. I won't tell. Good people. Food.
Water. Lots of news. Penny's got a baby. Homer's in love.
Both ready to jet. Both wondering. Both wondering. Happy
to be home.

Penny
Get him some water. You must be thirsty. Hungry too.

> Homer gets Odyssey Dog water and something to eat.

Homer
Dog's here. Hero ain't. That's plain enough. Them letters the
Missus got said the dog wouldn't never leave Hero's side.
Now here he is back all alone.

Penny
Tell us, Oddsee, how Hero died.

Odyssey Dog
Penny

Penny
Oddsee?

Odyssey Dog
Penny?

Penny
Must be hard for you. Knowing what you know. Tell it.

Odyssey Dog

The War continues on. The details, pretty much unspeakable. Who will win? Who can know?

The Runaway Slaves

Third: Win or lose
Means the same to us
As long as we're down here.
First: The Union won't reach this land any time soon.
Second: Unless the dog knows different.

Penny

And what of Hero? Is he dead? I know he's dead. Tell me how he died. I can bear it. Or if by some way he's living, hurry and tell me that.

Homer

He's dead. We know. But you tell it. We'll believe it coming from you. Go on.

Penny
Odyssey Dog
Homer

(Rest)

Odyssey Dog *(Aside)*

This is one of those moments we sometimes find ourselves in. I've got news and they want me to tell it. But the telling is hard because my news will make one sad and the other happy. I don't want to disappoint. It's a hard life when one wants to please. Why does life have to be like this? I'm just a dog.

The Runaway Slaves

First: Hearing how he died will help us.
Third: It will help you, Penny, to put him to rest.
Second: And our journey will gain speed when you free yourself from this place and all that's in it.

Homer
Tell it. Go head.

Penny
I can bear it. Hero's dead. How'd he die?

Odyssey Dog
It's a long story.
(Rest)
He told me how it was on the day he left. You all remember.
The Master gave Hero a uniform of his very own. It was grey
from top to bottom.

Penny
Oddsee.

Homer
Hero's dead, right?

Odyssey Dog
Boss-Master had a hat. And a feather from a bird. And
Hero had a pair of boots from the Boss-Master. The boots
he had were old. But they were still so nice. So nice, so nice
so nice, yep. So nice so pig leather and I so I so wanted to
chew on them because they were like the pig that had been
slaughtered and dressed and tanned and cut and sewn back
together to make those boots, it was like the pig was still
alive and you know how I would chase the pigs, when we
had pigs to chase. Chewing on those boots would have been
my pleasure. But I put my pleasure aside for the honor of
walking by my Master's side.

Penny
The Master is dead, right?

Odyssey Dog
Which one?

Homer
The Boss-Master, the Colonel, you know.

Odyssey Dog
When I say my Master of course I'm speaking of Hero. Him
and you all have a Master, but his and you all's Master is not
my Master. Although you could say that, because the Boss-
Master owns Hero who in turn owns me, you could figure that
the Boss-Master is in fact my Master. But he is not. Although,
the Great Master, the one who sits in the sky, you know, the
Great Master is Boss-Master's Master and Old-Hero's Master
and my Master too, but that Colonel-Boss-Master is not my
Master. When the Colonel called me, I would never ever come.

Penny
Oddsee. Tell me.

Odyssey Dog
I'm getting to it. Getting home was hard, and what I'm getting
to now is harder.
(Rest)
Old-Hero got me in as a pup, remember? Yep. Yep. Back
then I wasn't much to speak of. Funny eyes. Named me
Oddsee. Funny name. I grew to like it. Funny how you can
grow to like something like that.

Homer
Hero's dead. Just say it.

Odyssey Dog
I'm getting to it.

Homer
Taking the long way around.

Odyssey Dog
I'm getting to it. I'm getting to it. They told me how they
marched out of here, Old-Hero marching and the Master
riding that white horse named Fortune. Fortune was
prancing. Sounds like it was quite a sight. And they said,
Boss-Master's Missus, she cried as she waved goodbye and
you cried too Penny and Homer you just waved. Boss-Master
said he woulda took you along but what did the war need

with a man with only one foot, and besides you couldn't be trusted. What did the Rebels need with a rebel. Huh. Boss-Master was only going to take Hero because he could be trusted to stay by the Master's side at all times. Hero, yep, he was like me in that respect.

Homer
Is he alive or dead, dog?

Odyssey Dog
I'm getting to it. Don't kick me. Please.

Homer
Odyssey Dog

Penny
Go on.

Odyssey Dog
(Rest)
Sometimes the day was fine and the sun came out. Sometimes it rained. Sometimes there was—a mist.

Homer
A mist?!

Odyssey Dog
Like at Shiloh and Boss-Master, not Hero you understand, but Hero's Master, you understand, when he led a charge on his new Fortune and new Fortune fell down and the Boss-Master was going along so fast that I swear the Boss-Master kept charging right along, long after his new Fortune had fell out from underneath him. Boss-Master charging alone through the air.
(Rest)
Once there was a house. I forget where. There was a house with some women in it. They took turns sleeping. They were afraid. And they took turns sleeping and when they were awake they would sit with a rifle staring at the door. We found them there. Like the Three Fates that passed their one eye between them.

(Rest)

Hero, when he was Hero, he met a Yankee. With two blue
coats. The Yankee had a friend and the friend had a fever.
He told me how he got the Yankee's coat. Such a tall tall tale
I didn't believe his story for a minute. Anyhow. It was cold.
Even in the summer. Old-Hero put the blue coat underneath
his grey coat. Kept his own grey pants on though.

Homer
A Confederate from the waist down.

Penny
What?

The Runaway Slaves
He can read the signs.

Homer
What next, dog?

Odyssey Dog
Hero distinguished himself. And he took a new name.

Penny
Hero took a new name?

Odyssey Dog
In this one town, there was a slave gal. She sewed back
the buttons on Old-Hero's coat. I started to wonder when it
would end. I would dream of being back here. Some fellows
liked the War. Cannons be blazing! Towns be burnt! Food
was scarce. Hero shot a rabbit once.

Penny
And then he was shot!

Homer
Shot dead!

Penny
Go on and tell it! You hear me, just tell it!

Odyssey Dog

Master got another horse. Called him Salute. One day when
Salute was running and Master was charging and Old-Hero
was running alongside Master and I was running alongside
Old-Hero and we were all one fast moving cloud of black and
grey and me and I was thinking where the hell are we going
and will we ever get there? Then Old-Hero shouts, "Oh!"

Penny

And fell down dead.

Odyssey Dog

Master had been hit.

Homer

Hero?

Odyssey Dog

And Salute, not knowing any better just kept running.
And Old-Hero, Old-Hero—

Penny

Just say it! Just say it!

Odyssey Dog

Master lay there bleeding. Master stanched the wound. But.
No use. The War continues on. Came back with Master's
body, just arrived today. Missus is beyond consoling.

Penny

And my Hero: left dead on the field of battle for the birds to
eat out his eyes!

Homer

Hero's dead! God rest him!

Odyssey Dog

Old-Hero?
No.
He'll be home directly.

Penny
Home directly?

Odyssey Dog
I told it.

Homer
Home directly?

Penny
Home directly?

> Penny and Homer embrace. Both begin to cry.

Odyssey Dog *(Aside)*
Both are crying. I thought there'd be only one set of tears.

Penny
He's coming back? Don't lie to me.

Odyssey Dog
He's coming back.

Homer
Penny

The Runaway Slaves
First: We should go. Jet. Run.
Second: We should hide somewhere.
Third: From what they've said of Hero, how can we know we'll be safe?

Homer
It's not dark enough to travel yet. Still too much light in the sky.

Penny
I'll make him swear to keep your secret.

The Runaway Slaves
We thank you.

Penny
I'll run to meet him.

Homer
Stay here. Let him come in on his own.
Besides with the night coming and the road crawling
Crawling full of Patrollers,
It's safer to wait for him here.

Penny
You're right. I'll wait.

Homer
It's not dark enough. If it was, we could go.

Penny
You're still leaving.

Homer
And you'll stay.

Penny
I've got to stay now.

Homer
Alright.

Penny
But you'll be here when he comes. And you'll welcome him
with me. Then you'll go.

Homer
Then I'll go. Yeah.

Homer
Penny

Penny
I gotta go in and get things ready for him.
When he comes home things will be looking nice.

Homer

Not dark enough.
Not dark enough.
Not dark enough to jet.
Not yet.
If I could pull the dark up. From wherever it is.
It's in the east. Where just this morning
Everything looked possible and pleasant
Now things look dark.
Or take some of my own dark
And smear it against the sky
To block the sun out
Just long enough to make it just safe enough to go
Not dark enough
Not dark enough yet
Not dark enough yet to jet.

The Runaway Slaves

First: We could go now
Third: We could chance it
Second: We could throw caution to the wind
First: We could run
Third: We could just walk on by
Second: We could go, Homer
First: Help you ease your pain
Second: We'd be willing to risk it
Third: For you.

Homer

I want to be free
Not dead.
No, I'll wait.
It's just Hero I'll see.
I'll see them together and the sight will free me from this place.
And I'll head out with you, all the surer, and we'll travel all
    the faster.
Or maybe he won't even get here before nightfall

Maybe we'll already be on our way.
When him and Penny have their
Sweet reunion in the bed
Where she loved me but wouldn't
Love me.

Odyssey Dog
Old-Hero Old-Hero Old-Hero Old-Hero.

> Penny comes out of the house.
> She and Odyssey Dog run to greet the returning Soldier.

The Runaway Slaves
Second: The shape of a man
On the horizon.
Third: And closer and closer and closer he comes
First: Closer and closer and closer
First, Second and Third: The Hero.

> Penny reenters followed by Ulysses (formerly Hero).
> Odyssey Dog follows behind.

Penny
Close your eyes. Hold my hand. Keep them closed! Now
open them!

Ulysses
It looks the same.

Penny
It does. And so do you.

Ulysses
You're really here.

Penny
Yes.
(Rest)
Wrap your arms around me.

He wraps her in his arms.

Penny
Look at me, I'm dancing you!

She moves his arms, making him dance.
He lifts her up.

Ulysses
And I'm flying you.

Penny
I'm a bird!

They embrace. It's layered.

Penny
Ulysses

Ulysses
Old folks dead?

Penny
Me and Homer's all that's left. And now you.

Ulysses
Homer.

Homer
Hero.

Penny
"Ulysses"!

Homer
Like the Union General!?

Ulysses
That's right!

Homer
You didn't!

Ulysses
I did.

Penny
The nerve.

Ulysses
You like Ulysses alright?

Penny
I do, but what'll Missus say?

Ulysses
I'll tell her when the time is right. If I choose to.

Penny
It'll take me some getting used to.

Ulysses
Take as long as you need.
(Rest)
Strangers, huh?

The Runaway Slaves
Yes.

Ulysses
Runaways?

Homer
You'll keep their secret safe.

Ulysses
Alright.

Ulysses
Homer

(Rest)

Ulysses
Every day, every day, I'm telling you, I prayed to just have
the chance to come back here and show how I made good.
And here I am, girl. Here I am.

Penny
I'll get a good supper on directly.

Ulysses
Course you will.

Penny
Look at you. Just look at you. My feelings are all over the
place. I wish I was wearing something pretty.

Ulysses
You're pretty just like you are. Still just as pretty. Still just
as strong.
(Rest)
Old folks really dead?

Homer
Dead or sold off.

Ulysses
The Old Man's dead too? Well. Colonel would mention from
Missus' letters that someone had died or that someone had
got sold but he wouldn't never tell me who it was by name.

Penny
I told you I would wait for you.

Ulysses
You did.
(Rest)
Penny.

Penny
Hero.
(Rest)
"Ulysses."
I feel like you'll always be "Hero" to me.

Ulysses
Ulysses suits me and I chose it for myself. Any of you ever
done that? Choose your own name? No, right? It's really
something. Take all the time you need getting used to it.

Homer
Might take a lifetime.

Ulysses
Hopefully less than that.

Homer
Welcome home.

Ulysses
I thank you.

> Ulysses kneels on the ground. He gets up. He kneels again.

Ulysses
This is what I seen them do. When they get home. I'm just
following but it feels right.

> He kisses the ground.
> Then he sees Homer's writing.
> Homer erases the letters with his foot.

Ulysses
Homer

Ulysses
"Penny"?

Homer
I was just—

Penny
Look at you. Just look at you.

Ulysses
Just look at you.
(Rest)
Penny.

Penny
That's right.

Ulysses
And Oddsee came back to me alright. And he sure was my
luck cause here I am.

Odyssey Dog
Here I am. Here I am.

Ulysses
And he ran ahead like I told him. To tell you I was on my way.

Penny
Yes.

Ulysses
They're hanging black crepe at the Master's house. They'll
lay him in the ground tomorrow.

Homer
I suppose you'll help dig his grave.

Ulysses
I will. We'll dig it together.

Homer
Huh.
(Rest)
You're back. That's really something.

Ulysses
It's the War that's really Something, I'm telling you.

The Runaway Slaves

First: We'll be gone by nightfall.

Second: In case you're wondering.

Third: And we're good honest people.

First: Just like you.

Ulysses

We can't help you but so much.

The Runaway Slaves

Second: Not telling that we were ever here.

Third: And helping us hide until nightfall, that's kindness
enough.

First: And we, in turn, will keep your kindness secret.

Ulysses

We thank you.

(Rest)

I got stories. But I'll save them. So many stories. Most of
them unspeakable but I suppose in time I'll find a way to
tell. Like what I said to a Yankee when I met him face to
face. And other things. I'll be an old man on this porch
surrounded by his children telling war stories. I'll tell
everything to the children.

Penny

The children.

Ulysses

That'll be something, won't it?

(Rest)

How you been Homer?

Homer

I've been alright.

Ulysses

Working hard or hardly working?

Homer

Working hard.

Ulysses
And still here, huh?

Homer
Still here, yeah.

Ulysses
I brought home presents.

Homer
I'm gonna be heading out with them. Just so you know. We'd
go right this minute but—

Ulysses
You leaving with them?
You be safe, hear?
And I'll keep your secret.

Homer
That's your Word?

Ulysses
That's my Word.

Homer
Alright.

Ulysses
In the meantime gather round. I brought you something.
I brought you something too, Penny. Something for everybody.
Come on, gather round.

> They gather around Ulysses.
> He's like a king graciously holding forth.

Homer
Oddsee says it's a Yankee coat you wore underneath your
Rebel one.

Ulysses
You told them that, Oddsee?

Odyssey Dog
I did. I did.

Ulysses
Yeah, it's true. Take a look.

> He removes his Confederate Army coat,
> revealing the Union Army coat underneath.

Ulysses
It kept me good and warm, and, you know, it was a sort of
Truth for me.
(Rest)
Did Oddsee tell you how I freed a man?

Homer
You freed a man?

Ulysses
I did.

Odyssey Dog
Such a tall tall tale.

Ulysses
I really did.
(Rest)
But there'll be plenty of time to talk more about that. Plenty
of time for more stories.
(Rest)
Homer, this here's for you.

> From his satchel, he pulls out a foot, more like a shoe last,
> made of white alabaster.

Homer
A foot.

The Runaway Slaves
First: Not dark enough
Third: Not yet
Second: Not dark enough to jet.

Homer
A foot. I thank you.

Ulysses
They use it to model shoes on. The shop had burned to the ground. I seen it laying in the ash. Let it take the place of the one you lost.

Homer
I didn't lose it. Wasn't like I woke up one morning and couldn't remember where I put it.

Ulysses
Well, you know.
(Rest)
It's made of alabaster. It's worth a lot.

Homer
I thank you.

Ulysses
Homer

(Rest)

Ulysses
And for Penny:

From his satchel, he takes out a silver-tipped gardening spade.

Penny
A spade.

Ulysses
Silver-tipped.

Penny
Silver! It's lovely.

Ulysses

And you're only allowed to use it for your garden. And the garden's gonna have rules: I don't want you just planting vegetables with it. I want you to put some flowers in the ground too. Lots of flowers.

Penny

I knew you'd come home.

Ulysses

And here I am. I brought presents for everybody if they'd been here— A string of brass buttons! A shiny new spoon! The best present I brought is writ down right here.

> Ulysses takes a piece of paper from his breast coat pocket.
> He looks at it. Homer and Penny look on.

The Runaway Slaves
First: We can read.
Second: Show us.
Third: Or just tell us what it says.

Ulysses

I'll read it to you.

> But instead of reading it aloud he holds the paper close.
> He savors his power in the moment and their expectant looks,
> then decides to discuss another subject instead.

Ulysses
The Runaway Slaves
Homer
Penny
Ulysses

(Rest)

Ulysses

But first. Well, I brought something for Homer, and I brought something for you too, Penny. This here paper says something for all of us, but first, well, I brought something home for me too. Sit down, Penny.

Penny
Your presents gonna sweep me off my feet I wanna get swept.

Ulysses
Sit down.

Penny
Alright.

> Penny sits down. Ulysses takes a small photograph
> from his pocket. He looks at it before showing it to Penny.

Ulysses
Her name's Alberta. The Missus will bring her over here in a couple of days.

Penny
She's pretty. Who is she?

Ulysses
Alberta. She's a nice gal. Real nice.

Penny
Who is she aside from nice?

Ulysses
She's my new wife.

Penny
New—

Homer
New wife?

Penny
I'm— But I'm—

Ulysses
You and me, Penny, we don't have no kids. Can't, right?
You're still just as pretty still just as strong, but I was
thinking it would be good to have children. I was thinking—
I know you'll understand. You're good and true like that.

Alberta, she'll help you around here. When planting time
comes she'll do her part and work right along beside you.
And with Homer heading out, we'll need an extra hand.
She'll be a help to both of us.

Penny
But I'm—me.

Ulysses
And I'm giving you the better part of the deal, Penny. You
can't say that I'm not.

Penny
Hero. I mean—

Ulysses
I'm giving you the advantage in this. You're getting the
upper hand. I haven't told her about you. Not yet. And I won't.
Not until she gets here. You're hearing the news first. You
got the upper hand on it. So you can prepare yourself. And
by the time she gets here, Lord, you'll have it all figured out.
What her chores are and and and, and all the rest.

Homer
Where will she sleep?

Ulysses
That's not for you to ask.

Penny
Where will she sleep?

Ulysses
She'll sleep with me.
(Rest)
I went to the War and I came back here, I had to, but I didn't
have to, but I did, and not knowing who or what I'd find
waiting for me and so I did the best I could and just came
home with presents. I figured there's no sense in making it
all the way through and then come home to watch myself die
off. That's how I figured it, anyways.

Penny
That's how you figured it.

Ulysses
Yes.

Penny
You changed. You changed everything. Everything about
you went down the road. Where'd you go? Away. Now you're
back. But you're not back, are you?

Ulysses
I'm standing right here.

Penny
I'm right here too! And I'm still me. And I'm still living. And
I'm still here.

Ulysses
Put a good face on it, girl. Please.

Penny
The face I got isn't good enough, I guess. So I'll work on it.
Change it. Make it into something better. How about a smile?
All the days I waited for you. Smile. The months I waited
for you. Smile. All that time. And every time we heard of
someone dead I prayed it wasn't you. Smile. I worked hard
while you was gone. I minded the Missus like you told me to.
Like you told me to. Smile. Smile. Smile. I hate you.

> Penny cries. Homer comforts her.
> Ulysses watches Homer and Penny.
> He doesn't like what he's seeing.

Homer
We could go. Now.

Penny
Not me. No. And crying isn't gonna help. Why I thought
I deserved something special, I'll never know. I'll go inside

and make the house ready. For you and for your new bride.
You can count on me, Old-Hero, to do at least that.

She dutifully goes into the house.

The Runaway Slaves
First: You haven't heard the old stories
But I have.
Second: You don't know the old stories
But I do.
Third: Old stories, they guide us
Each its own North Star
You don't know them
And how could you?
Second: They happened so far back
First: Years ago
Third: Years and years ago
Second: Years and years and years ago
Third: What could they have to do with you?
Second: I'm scared of what will happen next.
The old story guides me to a dangerous place
A place I head to by homing habit.
Not like the journey I'm on now, right?
Third: The place I'm going now is Freedom
Second: But where is Freedom, really?
Will the air smell sweet?
Will the streets be paved with gold?
Will all in Freedomville welcome me with open arms?
Will there be food?
Will there be a bed to lay my Freedom Head?
First: Freedom will swell me, maybe
Maybe it will burst my brains to madness
Maybe it will flood my heart to death
Will I say, at the end of the day,
"God, I wish I'd stayed home?"
Second: I'm afraid of what will happen next.
Third: Inside, Penny makes up the marriage bed
And in doing so she takes her place in a long line of the
 Wronged.
Come out of the house, true wife, true love,

Second: Come with us
First: Come with us
Third: Come break the chain.
(Rest)
First: I wish it was dark enough
Third: I wish it was dark enough
Second: Dark enough to jet.
First, Second and Third: Not yet
Not yet
Not yet
Not yet.

Homer
It will be soon.

First Runaway
Homer help us
Come here and help us plan the way.
Let's ready ourselves together.

Homer
I'm figuring the best way for us. There's a kind of trick to
it. We gotta be looking for the signs all the time and in
everything. And if one way fails we gotta find another one.
That'll be the Way we go. I'll show you how we'll do it.

The Runaway Slaves
We thank you.

Homer joins The Runaway Slaves. They speak apart, making plans.
Ulysses, standing apart, speaks with Odyssey Dog.

Ulysses
He bothers me.
(Rest)
You saw him and her? Homer and Penny hugging together?

Odyssey Dog
I didn't see. I didn't see.

Ulysses
Yes you did. You're not blind.

Odyssey Dog
Penny cried. She's sad. Homer, he held her. They're friends.
That's all.

Ulysses
She wasn't faithful to me.

Odyssey Dog
Who can know? A hug is just a hug.

Ulysses
It tells me more than that. I know.

Odyssey Dog
You can't be sure. And besides. You weren't faithful either.

Ulysses kicks his dog.

Ulysses
Remember your place, dog.

Odyssey Dog
Ulysses

Odyssey Dog
Faithful, huh. You went to the War and you coulda been
anywhere. I looked for you. I smelled you out. The grass
was green and soft in some places and in other places it
was brown and crinkly. And I followed you and I found you.
That's faithful.
(Rest)
For me, faithful is easy. It's easy for a dog to be faithful.
Don't ask me why but it's true. Faithful for a dog comes
natural. Like to a man such as you comes walking upright.
Faithful is in a dog's bones. We're all born to do it. Can't
be broke. But for a man or a woman person, faithful comes
extra. Like speech comes extra for me. It's not a given.

And what is faithful, anyway, when there's a war on?
There's a home-way and a war-way. They're different.
Be kind, Old-Hero. Be kind. You're home.

Ulysses
He bothers me. Cause of Penny? Maybe. Or maybe that's
just the start of it.

Odyssey Dog
Leave it. Leave it.

Ulysses
Homer?

> Homer steps away from The Runaway Slaves
> to speak with Ulysses.

Homer
We'll be gone soon, if you're wondering.

Ulysses
Did you sleep with my wife?

Homer
Your picture wife?

Ulysses
Penny, I'm talking about.

Homer
It's Penny who should be in that picture. Not that other gal.

Ulysses
Did you love my Penny yes or no?

Homer
She needed someone. She chose me. She needs someone
now, but you've moved on. How you gonna bear that? How
she's gonna bear that, I don't know. But it's not my place to
know. My place is somewhere better. And she's staying here
with you cause she's true like that, all right?

Ulysses
Yeah. Go on then.

Homer
Tell me something.

Ulysses
What.

Homer
Did he ever get around to freeing you?

Ulysses
No. He didn't.

Homer
Ulysses

Ulysses
He didn't give me my freedom.
(Rest)
Not even with his dying breath.
In spite of all his promises.
And what beautiful promises they were.
With every day they grew fuller and riper.
I'd imagine sitting at a head of a fine table and eating my fill
That's how real they were. I could taste them.
And when I'd wake up my mouth was only full of my own teeth
And tongue and spit. And my stomach growled.
And he'd feed it. With promises. And I would feast on them.
I don't take after him in looks but I did take after him.
I did. I did. Following in his every footstep.
My stride got to be the same as his.
And sometimes I'd hear myself laughing and think, that's
      the Colonel,
No that's me.
Can you imagine? Can you see it?
I should have killed him.
I had the chance more than once but didn't.
And when he finally died

I thought for a minute I'd follow him into the grave
That's how close we were.
You,
You make me think of how I wronged you. Just like with me
and Master:
I'd always, just by being myself, I'd always be somehow
reminding him
Of his Faults against me.
And so, to make it all right, to make it bearable, so I could
find a way to breathe
I went and I cut out my soul.
I cut my soul out of myself.
And I gave it up to him.
Or I lost it.
You're lucky. You're going to a better place.

Homer
Freedom's better than this.

Ulysses
How you know for sure? How you know?

Homer
I just know, that's all. In my heart. I know.

Ulysses
It's dark enough, Homer. You better get going. Go on to that
better place and go there quick.

> Ulysses takes out his knife. He lunges at Homer,
> intent on killing him. They struggle.

Homer
No!

The Runaway Slaves
No! No!

Odyssey Dog
No!

Penny
No!!!

Penny
Ulysses

(Rest)

Penny
No.

Penny
Ulysses
Homer
Penny

(Rest)

Ulysses
Penny

Ulysses withdraws his knife.

Penny
All that time of waiting and wishing and praying that you
    were alive
And I was in our house just now
Praying you was dead.
And all those times I would lay with you
Praying you was him.
God must not of heard me right.
My prayers got confused.
My prayers got confused.

The Runaway Slaves
First: Now the sun is down
The day has pulled a blanket over its own head
Third: Wish us good luck

First: Wish us good fortune
Second: Wish us safety
First: Wish us food and water along the way
Third: Wish us Freedom
Second: Wish us open arms when we arrive
First: Wish us work. Wish us luck
Third: Wish us a way to get our families back
Second: Wish us at least that. Wish us at least that.

Homer
We're heading out. We'll go.

Penny
Yes. We'll go.

Ulysses
You'll stay, Penny. Please. I don't want you going.

> Ulysses takes Penny's hand but Penny pulls away.
> She tears a piece from her dress, handing it to Ulysses.

Penny
I'm leaving. I'm gone. Let's go.

> Penny leaves with Homer and The Runaway Slaves.
> Ulysses and Odyssey Dog are alone.

Odyssey Dog
There are worse things. I dunno what but there are worse things.

Ulysses
Ulysses
Ulysses

> Ulysses takes that paper out, looks it over.

Ulysses
This paper. I never got to read it to them.
The Proclamation. I copied it down.

(Rest)
It says we're free.

Odyssey Dog
The Runaways, they still got to run.

Ulysses
Still and all.
(Rest)
These are my hands now.
(Rest)
I'll bury the Boss-Master.

Odyssey Dog
I'll help.

Ulysses looks toward Boss-Master's house,
ready to undertake his new life.
Odyssey Dog holds the spade.

End of Play

DARK IS THE NIGHT

Suzan-Lori Parks
transcribed by Steven Bargonetti

Allegro (bluesy) ♩ = 147

Voice

Guitar

E5   E5

Gtr.

DARK IS THE NIGHT   LONG IS THE DAY -

Gtr.

DARK IS THE NIGHT -   LONG IS THE DAY -

Gtr.

- GOT TIME FOR WORK -   NO TIME TO PRAY -

HE'S LEAVING

Suzan-Lori Parks
transcribed by Steven Bargonetti

Andante (Doubletime country blues, rockabilly feel) ♩ = 93

BUT HE KNOWS HE CAN NOT STAY.   THE GAL HE LOVES SHE'S MA-KING PER-

guitar simile

-FUME   PER - FUME WHEN   SHE   WA - LKS

THE GAL HE LOVES - SHE'S MA-KING   PER-FUME WHEN SHE WALKS-

-   -   -   I WOULD-N'T NE-VER CROSS HER, THOUGH MM-MM

SHE'LL CUT   YOU   LIKE   A   HAWK___

PASSING THE TIME

The Colonel's Song
(repeat for each verse)

Suzan-Lori Parks

Like a Cowboy Song

The Colonel

(cowboy swing -starts freely)

I'VE SAT ON_____ A MOUN-TAIN_ I'VE SAT ON_____ A HILL I LOVE GOD_____ AND COUN-TRY_____ I PAY ALL_ MY BILLS - - I'M A PRET-TY_____ GOOD HUS - BAND, THOUGH DON'T ASK_ MY WIFE IF SHE CAT - CHES ME HERE, I'LL PAY WITH MY LIFE.

THIS BRIGHT WILDERNESS

Suzan-Lori Parks

transcribed by Steven Bargonetti

MISPLACED MYSELF
Odyssey Dog's Theme

Suzan-Lori Parks
transcribed by Steven Bargonetti

HERO'S THEME

Suzan-Lori Parks
transcribed by Steven Bargonetti

PENNY'S THEME

Suzan-Lori Parks
transcribed by Steven Bargonetti

LEAVE ALL THIS BEHIND
Runaway's Theme

Suzan-Lori Parks
transcribed by Steven Bargonetti

(repeat sections as needed)

slight bend

KISS

Suzan-Lori Parks
transcribed by Steven Bargonetti

OLD STORIES

Suzan-Lori Parks
transcribed by Steven Bargonetti

keep repeating, rit. and fade........

PASSING INTO WILDERNESS

Suzan-Lori Parks
transcribed by Steven Bargonetti

BRONZE STAR THEME

Suzan-Lori Parks
transcribed by Steven Bargonetti

HOMER'S THEME

Suzan-Lori Parks
transcribed by Steven Bargonetti

Andante (Funky Feel)

Named one of *TIME* magazine's "100 Innovators for the Next New Wave," in 2002 Suzan-Lori Parks became the first African American woman to receive the Pulitzer Prize in Drama for her Broadway hit *Topdog/Underdog*. A MacArthur "Genius" Fellowship recipient, she has also been awarded grants by the National Endowment for the Arts, the Rockefeller Foundation, the Ford Foundation, the New York State Council on the Arts and the New York Foundation for the Arts. She is the recipient of a Lila Wallace–Reader's Digest Award, a CalArts/ Herb Alpert Award in the Arts (Theatre) for 1996 and a Guggenheim Foundation Fellowship. She is an alumna of Mount Holyoke College and New Dramatists.

Her numerous plays include *Father Comes Home From the Wars* (2015 Pulitzer Prize finalist, 2015 Edward M. Kennedy Prize for Drama Inspired by American History, 2014 Horton Foote Prize), *The Book of Grace*, *Topdog/ Underdog* (2002 Pulitzer Prize), *In the Blood* (2000 Pulitzer Prize finalist), *Venus* (1996 OBIE Award), *The Death of the Last Black Man in the Whole Entire World*, *Fucking A*, *Imperceptible Mutabilities in the Third Kingdom* (1990 OBIE Award for Best New American Play) and *The America Play*. Parks's work on *The Gershwins' Porgy and Bess* earned the production a Tony

PHOTO BY TAMMY SHELL

Award for Best Revival of a Musical in 2012. In 2007 her *365 Plays/365 Days* was produced in more than seven hundred theaters worldwide, creating one of the largest grassroots collaborations in theater history. Her work is the subject of the PBS Film *The Topdog Diaries*.

Suzan-Lori's first novel, *Getting Mother's Body*, was published by Random House in 2003.

Her first feature-length screenplay was *Girl 6* written for Spike Lee. She's also written screenplays for Brad Pitt, Denzel Washington, Jodie Foster and Oprah Winfrey, adapting Zora Neale Hurston's classic novel *Their Eyes Were Watching God*, which premiered on ABC's Oprah Winfrey Presents. As a film actor Parks has appeared in the fictional-documentary *The Making of Plus One*, which premiered at the Cannes Film Festival in 2009.

In November 2008 Suzan-Lori Parks became the first recipient of the Master Writer Chair at The Public Theater. At The Public, and as she tours the country, she performs her innovative performance piece, Watch Me Work, a play with action and dialogue/a meta-theatrical writing class. She also serves as a visiting arts professor in dramatic writing at New York University's Tisch School of the Arts.

Holding honorary doctorates from Brown University, among others, Suzan-Lori credits her writing teacher and mentor, James Baldwin, for starting her on the path of playwriting. One of the first to recognize Parks's writing skills, Mr. Baldwin declared Parks "an astonishing and beautiful creature who may become one of the most valuable artists of our time."